Transcend

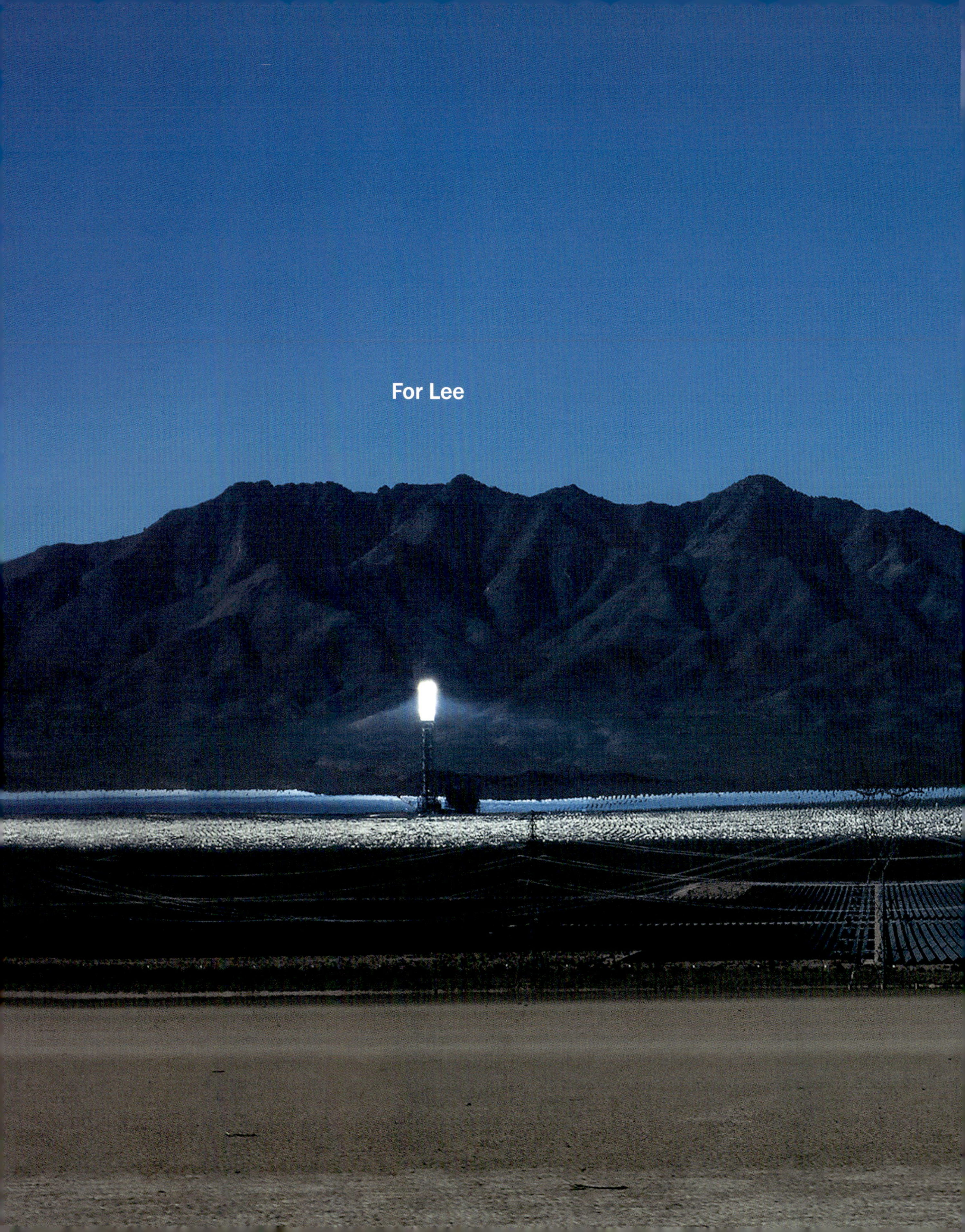

For Lee

Transcend

Freedom to Love

Sandra Chen Weinstein

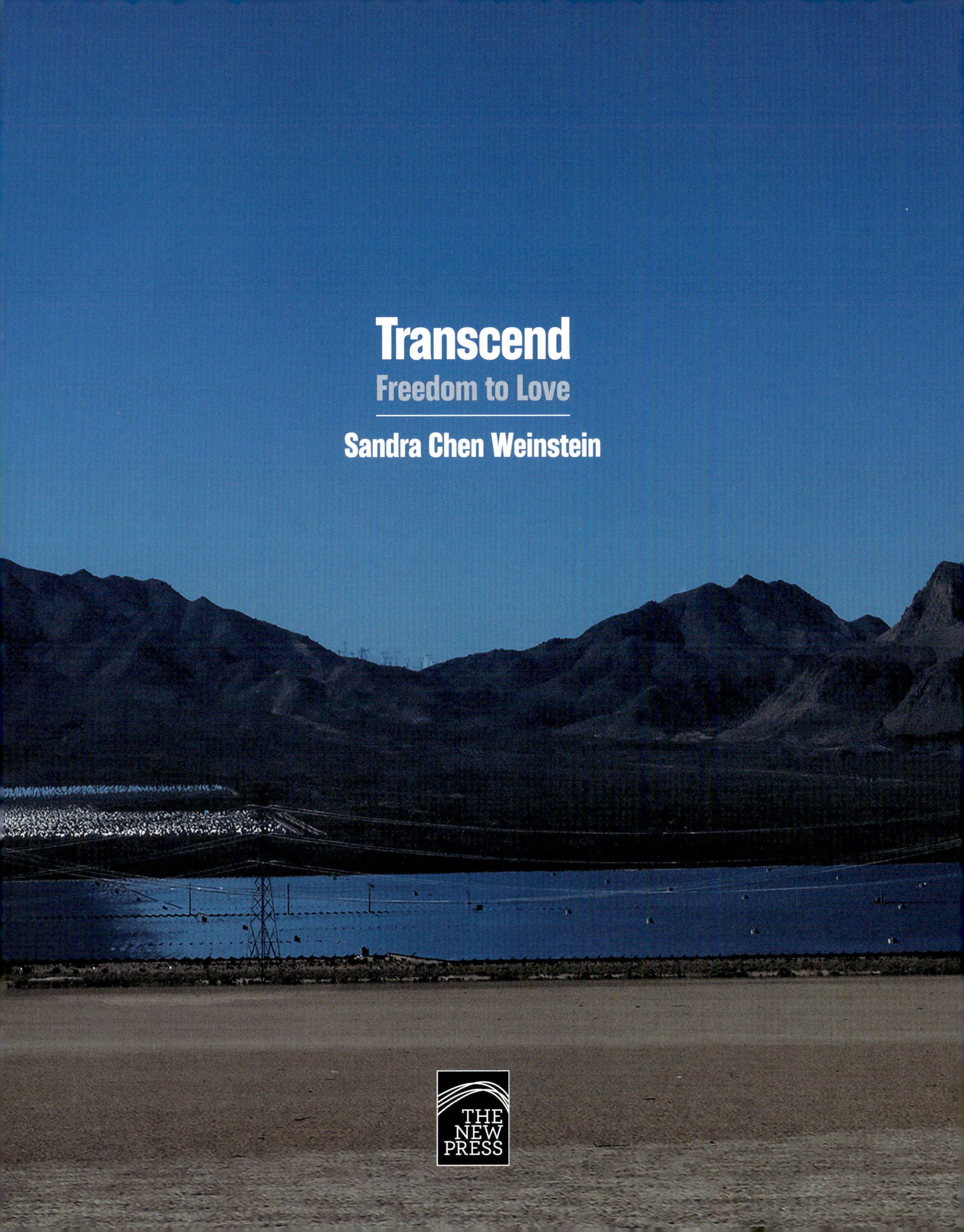

THE NEW PRESS

Published in the United States by The New Press, New York, 2024
Distributed by Two Rivers Distribution

ISBN 978-1-62097-793-4 (pb)
ISBN 978-1-62097-827-6 (ebook)
CIP data is available

The New Press publishes books that promote and enrich public discussion and understanding of the issues vital to our democracy and to a more equitable world. These books are made possible by the enthusiasm of our readers; the support of a committed group of donors, large and small; the collaboration of our many partners in the independent media and the not-for-profit sector; booksellers, who often hand-sell New Press books; librarians; and above all by our authors.

www.thenewpress.com

Book design and composition © 2024 by Emerson, Wajdowicz Studios (EWS)
This book was set in FranklinGothic URW, Helvetica, Hiragino Sans, Rama Gothic, and Zapf Dingbats
Front cover image: Carmen | San Francisco, CA | 2016

Printed in the United States of America

10 9 8 7 6 5 4 3 2 1

Preface

JON STRYKER

This photobook series project was born out of conversations that I had with Jurek Wajdowicz. He is an accomplished art photographer and frequent collaborator of mine, and I am a lover of and collector of photography. I owe a great debt to Jurek and his design partner, Lisa LaRochelle, in bringing this book series to life.

Both Jurek and I have been extremely active in social justice causes—I as an activist and philanthropist and he as a creative collaborator with some of the household names in social change. Together we set out with an ambitious goal to explore and illuminate the most intimate and personal dimensions of self, still too often treated as taboo: sexual orientation and gender identity and expression. These books continue to reveal the amazing multiplicity in these core aspects of our being, played out against a vast array of distinct and varied cultures and customs from around the world.

Photography is a powerful medium for communication that can transform our understanding and awareness of the world we live in. We believe the photographs in this series will forever alter our perceptions of the arbitrary boundaries that we draw between others and ourselves and, at the same time, delight us with the broad spectrum of possibility for how we live our lives and love one another.

We are honored to have Sandra Chen Weinstein as a collaborator in *Transcend*. She and the other photographers in this ongoing series are more than craftspeople: they are communicators, translators, and facilitators of the kind of exchange that we hope will eventually allow all the world's people to live in greater harmony. ■

Jon Stryker, philanthropist, architect, and photography devotee, is the founder and board president of the Arcus Foundation, a global foundation promoting respect for diversity among peoples and in nature.

The Power of Us

CAROL McCUSKER, PH.D. (SHE/HER)

Not everything that is faced can be changed, but nothing can be changed until it is faced.—James Baldwin[1]

I contain multitudes.—Walt Whitman[2]

A photographic portrait is in essence a block of light made in about 1/100th of a second. Within it, a sitter collaborates with the photographer in pose, expression, clothing, place. Together they create a record of an individual staking a claim for themselves in the present as witness for the future. They are growing an image archive of now. History is full of such portraits; we are drawn to them for what they tell us about human nature and cultures then and now. They break open barriers and hearts, alter our prejudices, and act as remembrance—important themes in the book you now hold in your hands.

James Baldwin warns us that if invisibility prevails nothing can change. Regarding photographic portraits, his quote is prescient and literal: the power of actual faces, facing outward, to face the world revealing their lives, here to stay. Even though 1/100th of a second is unlikely to reveal the complexities of a human soul, it provides a compelling threshold. Together, Sandra Chen Weinstein and her subjects sit together to reveal something of their inner lives at the moment of the camera's "click." The result is a tender solidarity as photographer and the photographed become not only kin but more of who they each are.

But what are portraits ultimately for, and can they convey more than facts? They give light and substance, for sure. Yet, the best of Sandra's photographs creates an arc to the ineffable and the inevitable (she is a kind of shaman with her camera). Consider her photographs from Palestine, India, and the Arab Spring, or photographs of Native Americans or asylum seekers in Houston, Texas. These are revelatory of Sandra's commitment to be a witness, yet from a respectful distance. With *Transcend*, however, she has hit her mark, no less because it is a deeply personal project that dovetails our present zeitgeist.

Sandra is originally from Taiwan and has lived in many countries working for the American Foreign Service. She knows how it feels to be an outsider. She has spent years quietly fusing her curiosity about people and the world with her love of photography and travel. These are healing occupations that facilitate connection. Sandra, more than most of us, has become a global citizen. Especially with *Transcend*, for which she chose people she met through her work, friends, family, and activists in her own or her child's wider circle. Each are photographed here in environments where they felt most safe.

Portrait photographers work hard to make their sitters feel at ease. Some prefer to be in their own environment using natural light; for others, a planned studio session with backdrops and light diffusers help them best express themselves. With LGBTQ+ visibility long denied, Sandra has created a witness to sensual bodies infinitely wild, polyglot, expansive. We see queer culture from Taiwan, Iceland, Australia, the United States, and Japan, and people of every age, color, and shape. Some sit quietly against a dark background. A few hold who and what they love—a partner, a mother, a tree, a pet.

Among the most moving to me are a few of the "solitaries": the Byronic beauty and self-possessed "David Iñiguez" and the solidly hip "Sadie" (both from Reykjavík), and the beautifully lit "Ari" from San Francisco. Mr. Chi Chia-Wei personifies the wisdom and sacrifice of his generation, an example for younger LGBTQ+ communities, since so many of the male elders that should-be-here have succumbed to the AIDS epidemic. He gently communes with an ancient tree as does the serene "Lee" on this book's back cover. Portraits of couples, "Jon and Mikael" and "Barbara and Jess," I want to know them! These are tender, integrated messages, portraits that express fluid identities, loving, empowering, and embodying a complicated global humanity.

This book is born out of love for Sandra Chen Weinstein's own child, Lee, who came out as trans in 2016. Yet Sandra has been committed to photographing the LGBTQ+ community since 2008; several of her series, *Metamorphosis, She/They,* and *American Pride*, are testimony. Her intentions are clear: to celebrate the queer community and to address and assuage the fear and loneliness within it. She follows photographer Sebastião

Salgado's empathetic perspective when photographing people, "If you take a picture of a human that does not make him noble, there is no reason to take this picture." This is what photographic portraits do best; we recognize or reconcile ourselves and our potential in the other through empathy and respect for all our visible humanness, including our postures, chipped nail polish, jewelry choices, T-shirt messaging ("I AM BIG," "Strong enough," "Our Lives Matter"). All are portals to the sitter's inner life and our own, a prerequisite to love.

The number of portraits of women, BIPOC, and more recently, LGBTQ+ people has increased in the twenty-first century, with each insisting on their place in the pantheon of notable histories. This is not a new phenomenon; centuries ago, gay, bi-sexual, intersex, or trans people were frequently rendered in painted portraits. Look at historical paintings and prints from Asia, the Middle East, or Europe, from ancient Egypt, Greece, or Rome through the Renaissance into the 19th century. They are portrayals of non-binary individuals. But as the institutions of empire, government, religion, and industry globally intensified and unified in the nineteenth century, white, male "authorities" asserted their raw power. Their dominance depended on control. From the Enlightenment to the present, an enforced conformity has been like a zealot's fist over the rural and urban, the poor and middle-classes, women, and POC. So why has LGBTQ+ visibility become more visible recently when it existed openly in centuries past? Suffice it to say that conservative trends come and go and must vilify expressions of difference where and when it can in the name of power, especially when it is most threatened. That time is now.

Photographs in and of themselves are intrinsically silent, but they are *not* quiet. They contain worlds. Quiet, for poet Kevin Quashie, is highly expressive. He explores photographs of Black history to better see their often-overlooked interiorities. The camera's fraction of a second can make thinking and feeling visible. Manifested from somewhere inside the person photographed, it is there in the fold of two people's shoulders leaning on one another, the grip of hands, or eyes that barely conceal shyness or pain. Gay culture in the media is often portrayed as flamboyant, elated, dramatic, loud, colorful (Quashie notes the same for Black culture). This can lead us to miss what else is there: a vibrant, voluptuous inner life, quiet yet strong, pushing outward into a new world, vulnerable and powerful. Instead of visualizing stereotypes, i.e., angry, resistant, Quashie suggests states of "waiting . . . surrender . . . dreaming . . . into the quiet . . . It can remind us of the wealth of humanity."[3]

Consider the following words from Walt Whitman's *I Sing the Body Electric*. As a gay man himself, they are full of Whitman's love toward all humanity. He saw himself as one with the human flow of life with no self-pity, no alienating boundaries—a multitude together:

To be surrounded by beautiful, curious, breathing, laughing flesh is enough,
To pass among them or touch any one, or rest my arm ever so lightly round his or her neck for a moment, what is this then?
I do not ask any more delight, I swim in it as in a sea.
There is something in staying close to men and women and looking on them, and in the contact and odor of them, that pleases the soul well,
All things please the soul, but these please the soul well.[4]

Whitman had a profound love for human nature, which cannot be singularly defined or constrained. What would be most interesting to see going forward is this: a re-photographic project of the people in this book, perhaps in 2040, to see not only how the world had changed in fifteen years but what their lives had become and who they touched in the becoming, as parents, teachers, artists, mayors, scientists, health care providers, presidents, innovators.[5] The sum power of us. We contain multitudes. ■

1 James Baldwin, *As Much Truth as One Can Bear*, January 14, 1962, *New York Times*.
2 Walt Whitman, "Song of Myself" (stanza 51), *Leaves of Grass*, 1855.
3 Kevin Quashie, Ph.D., *The Sovereignty of Quiet* (Rutgers, 2012), paraphrased. To hear Quashie speak about the sovereignty of quiet, see Smith College's *Scholars in Studio* video: https://www.youtube.com/watch?v=m7wlYcRv2xl
4 Walt Whitman, "I Sing the Body Electric" (stanza 4), *Leaves of Grass*, 1855. Whitman's *Leaves of Grass* was a life-long project for the poet not unlike many photographers who work with a series of images over many years. His 1855 first edition contained just twelve poems. He reworked and expanded it for almost four decades, republishing it many times until his death in 1892. Up to nine editions of *Leaves of Grass* exist, the last containing 400 poems.
5 May Sandra Chen Weinstein have time to rework and expand her project as Walt Whitman did his *Leaves of Grass*, creating a satisfying deep-time record of our age. Sites of further interest: Sandra Chen Weinstein photography: http://www.sandrachenphoto.com/. Queer art history: https://abirpothi.com/11-famous-paintings-in-art-history-that-depict-queer-love/

Austin | San Jose, CA | 2016

"I am twelve. Looking in the mirror, this is *not* who I am. Will people accept the true me? Why do people hate me. Why do Christians suddenly hate me? Have we even met? I will be my authentic self. Acceptance, gratitude, love—I wish it was like this for all of us. *Everyone* needs to be loved!"

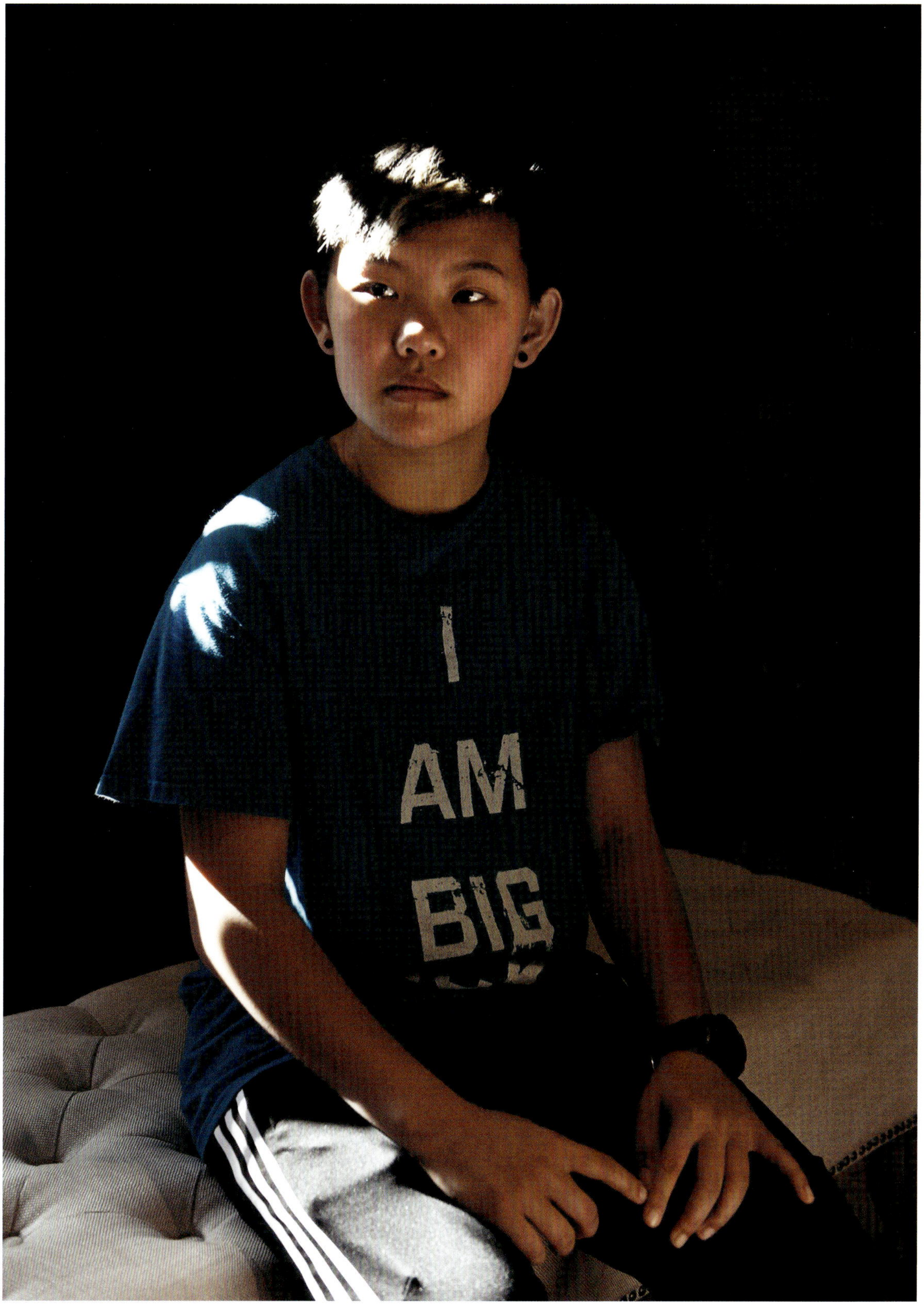
I
AM
BIG

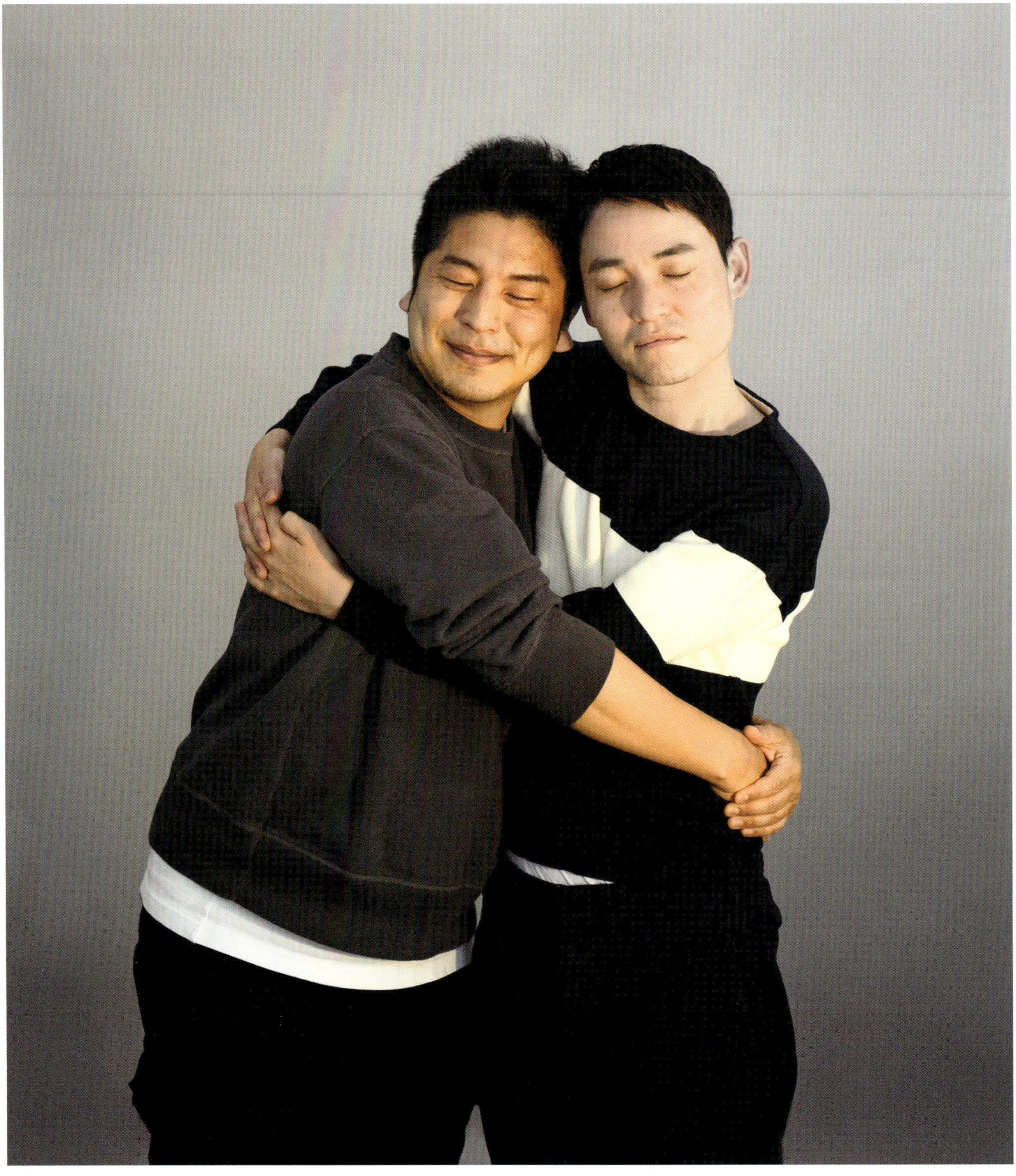

Love, Tokyo | Tokyo, Japan | 2019

Asher and Hart
San Francisco, CA | 2016

"From birth I was told who I was. I was constantly fed a steady diet of expectations assigned to my gender. Desperate to gain sustenance despite the rules and limits presented to me, I pushed and pulled in every direction, looking for comfort and acceptance. My stomach was in knots when forced into a dress. I often found relief in make-believe and Halloween costumes. Top hats, ties, sweater vests, and capes fed my soul, but the real world was always waiting for me when it came time to put everything away. Transitioning allowed me to break free from that box and feast on life outside its confines."—Asher

"He's just an absolute marvel to me. I had some struggles for a while when I would look at old photographs and get teary-eyed."
— Asher's mother, Hart

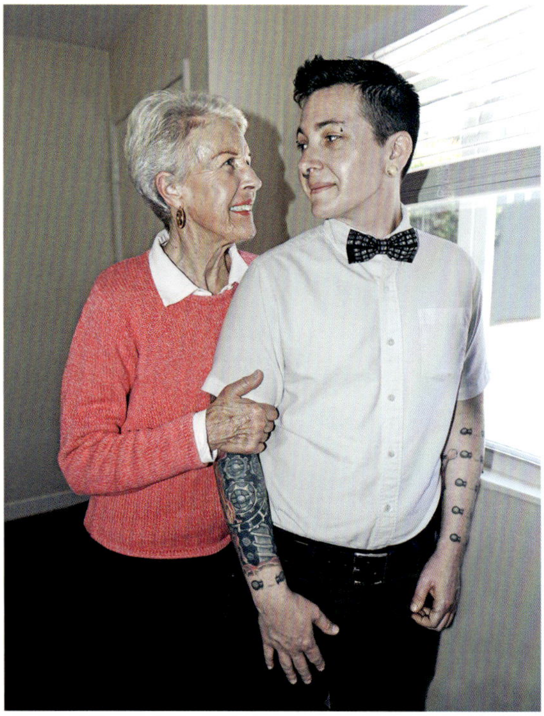

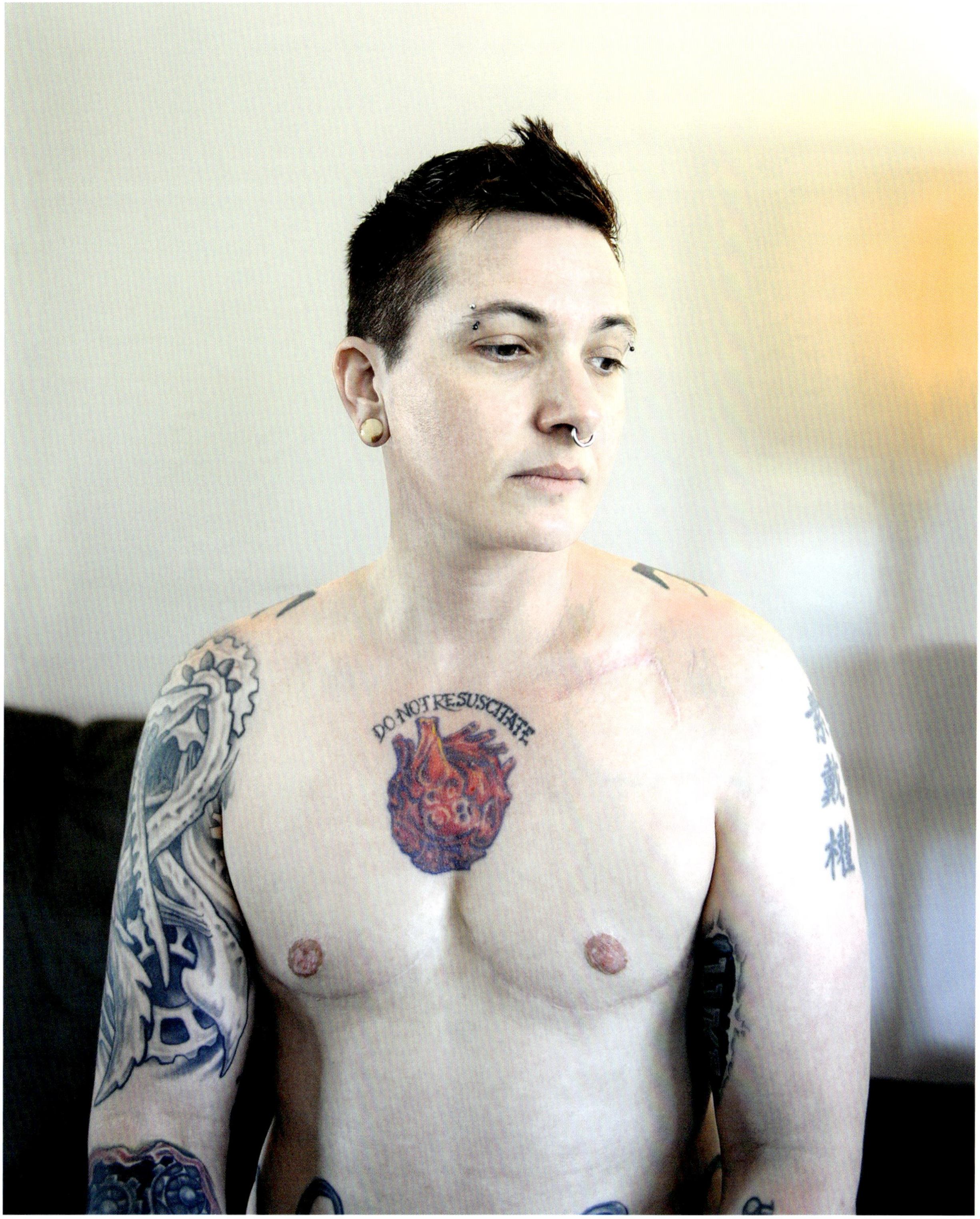
DO NOT RESUSCITATE

Olivia | San Francisco, CA | 2016

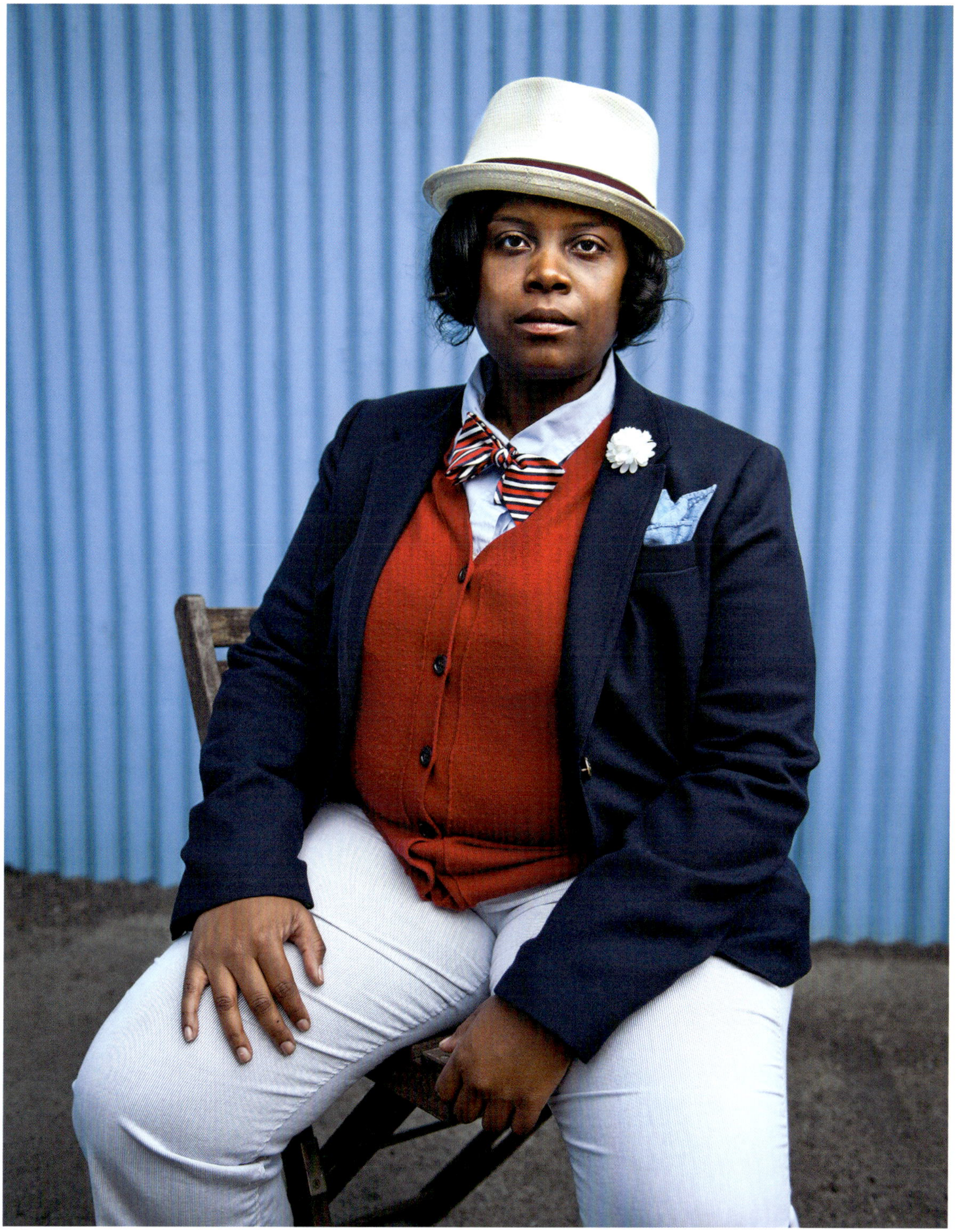

Strong Enough | San Francisco, CA | 2016

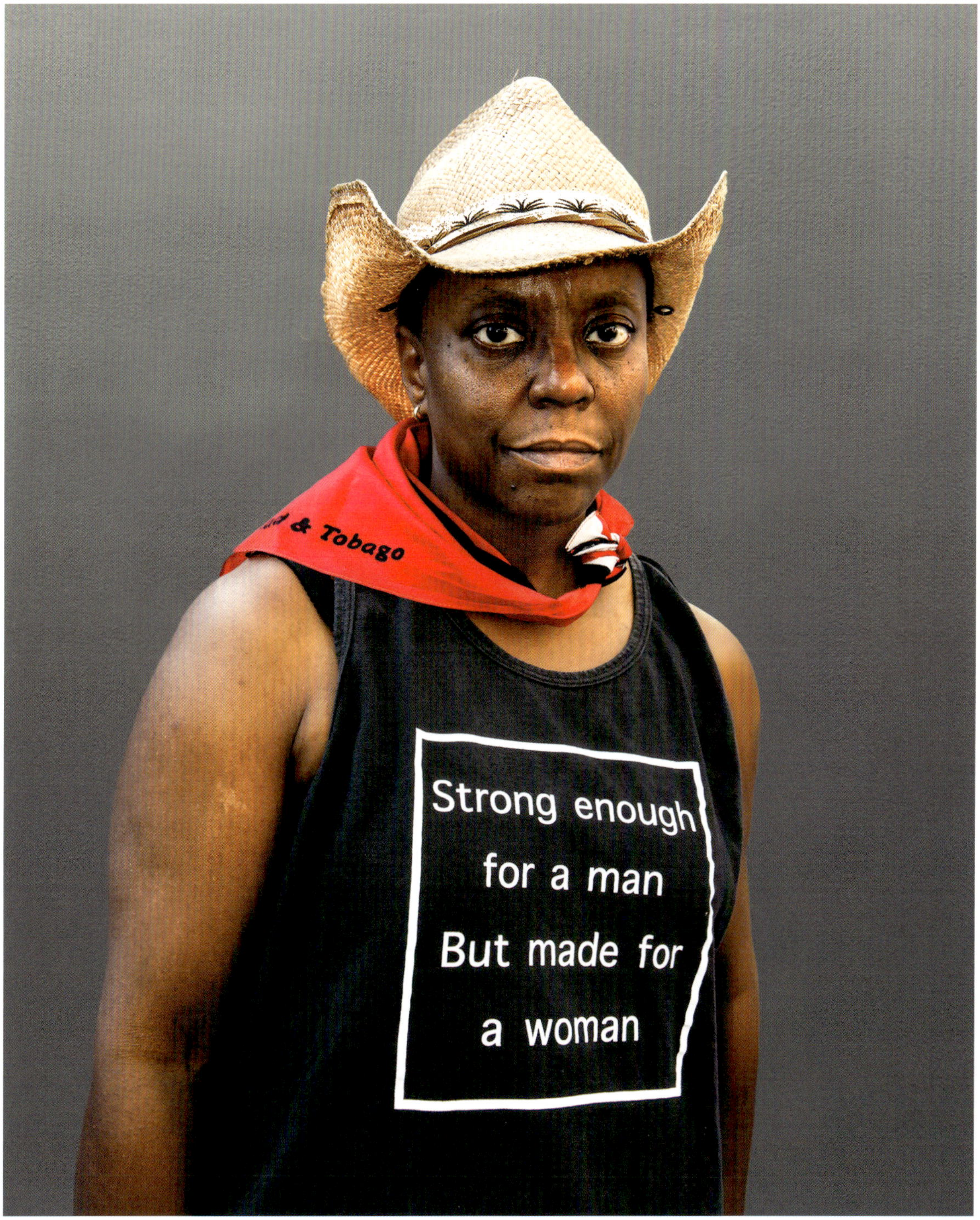
& Tobago
Strong enough
for a man
But made for
a woman

Jon and Mikael (right) | San Francisco, CA | 2016

"After twenty-five years living in the U.S.A., it's now time to return to my homeland in Melbourne, Australia, with the love of my life, my American husband for more than twenty years." —Jon

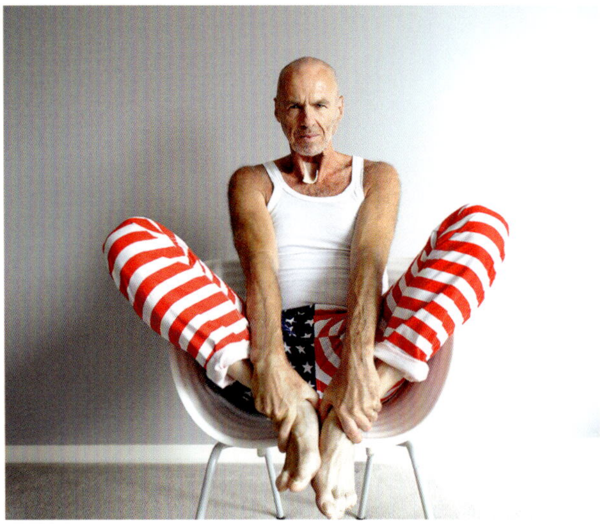

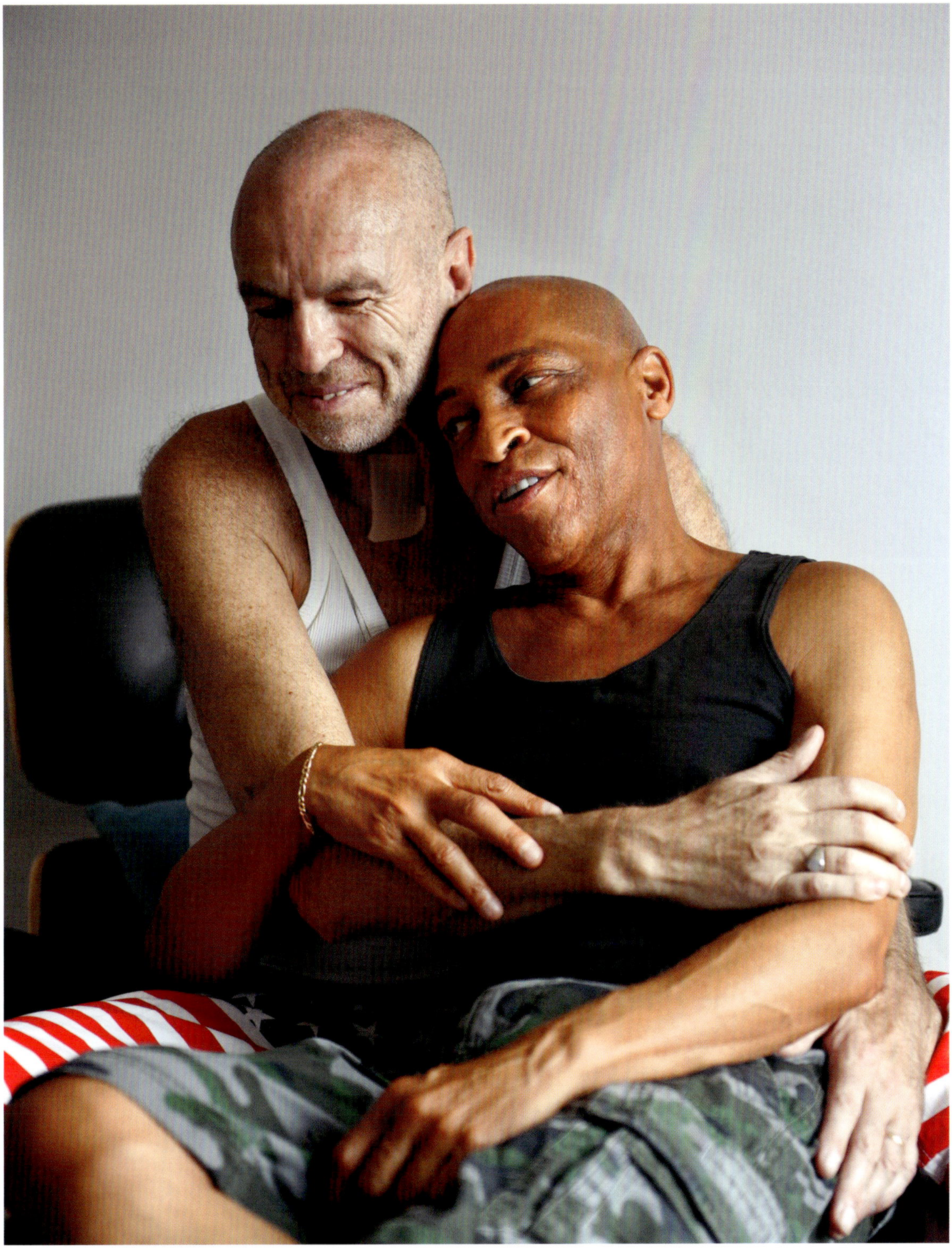

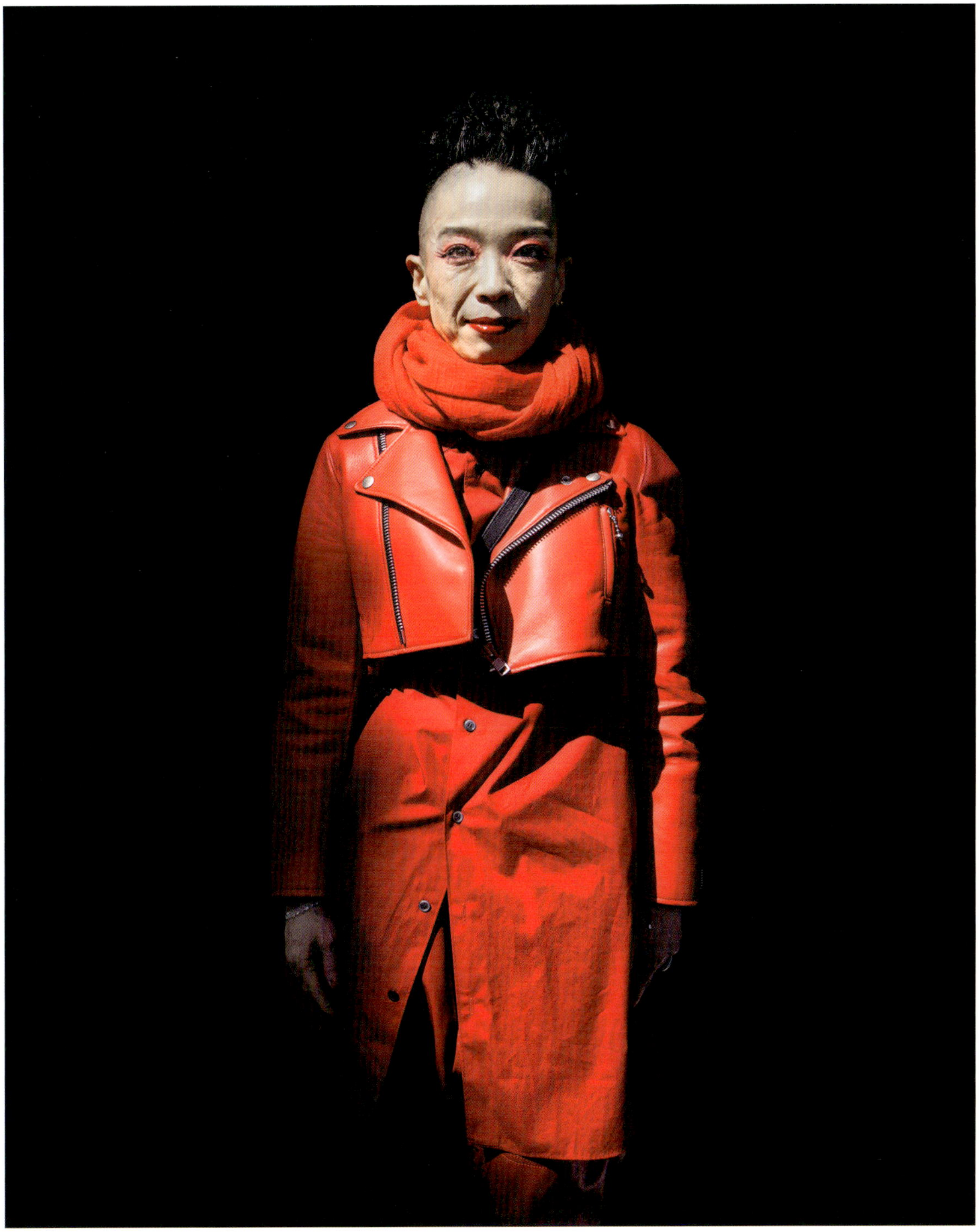

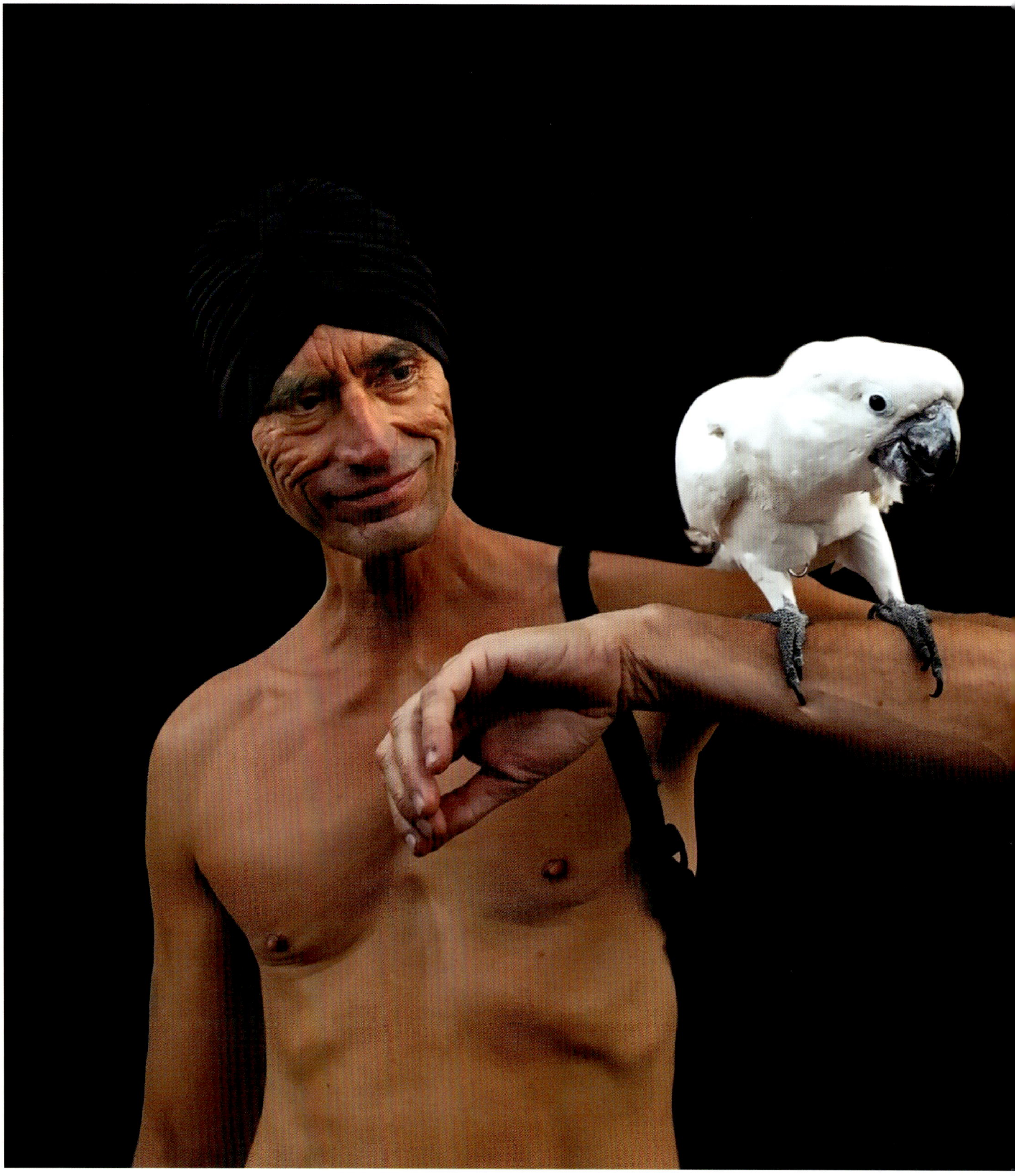

Jack and his cockatoo
San Francisco, CA | 2016

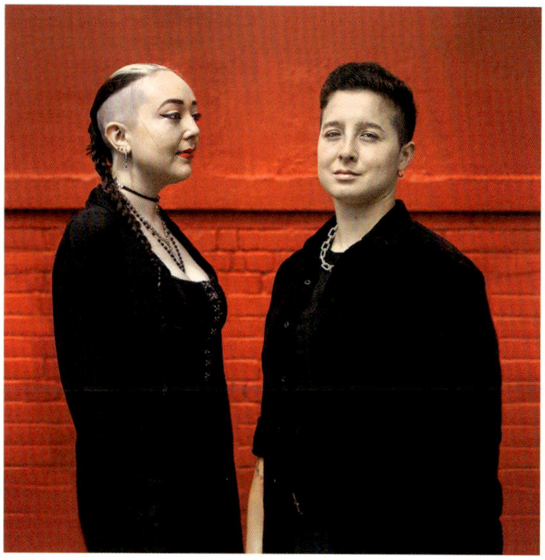

"I am grateful to be queer and to have queer love in my life. I feel freedom and true joy through queer community. I was taught that God condemns queer people, but queerness is how I connect to love. Love is a gift that makes life worth living. I am happy as I am and I want to be here, alive, in love, and celebrating the beautiful people around me."— Amara

"Growing up, I had always been interested in women. I had crushes and felt so awkward around my female friends and classmates. It became clear when I was in seventh grade that I was gay. I had started having a romantic relationship with a girl on my softball team and wanted to be able to tell people—which meant I had to tell my parents too.

I first told my brother. He didn't care or say much really—he was 14 years old and preoccupied with his own life—and we spent the night on Facebook looking at what girls we thought were cute. Then I told my Dad, during a car ride. I was so terrified, I was sweating, and he just made stupid dad jokes about it.

Lastly, I told my mom. It didn't go well. I truly believe she had less of an issue with me liking women than she did with me being masculine. I also felt that, with the way she was raised and where we lived, she feared for my safety and ability to live an "easy" life. What I chose was hard in her eyes. We had a relationship filled with turmoil for quite a while. Neither of us would back down. She wouldn't let family give me money to buy masculine clothes, and I was spiraling hard into depression and rebellion. I was being bullied viciously at school during this time as well for being gay, and my isolation was leading me into a dark place.

My dad started to notice and decided that I needed a person in my corner before something horrible happened. He took me to a LGBTQ center that had a youth program where I met other queer teens. This became a safe haven for me and I don't know what would have become of me without it. He also took me shopping in secret for men's clothes because I really wanted them.

Over time my mom came around. She would look at the resources I brought home from the LGBTQ center, and began to learn about what being LGBTQ was like. She realized how troubled I was with the state things had come to and how she would not be able to keep me in her life otherwise. Today my mom is one of my biggest supporters, buying me my favorite cologne, giving my partner gifts and inviting her to stay in our family home, and just loving and accepting who I am. We had this journey together and she's one of my best friends.

I'm very fortunate that my family has been able to grow and come so far. Without them I would have drowned under societal pressure and horrendous school bullying. I'm happy now, and they helped me get to where I currently am. I now get to live in a city with other queers, have amazing friends, a lovely partner, pets, and this total fulfilled life I couldn't have dreamed of as a kid. I just get to live my most authentic queer life filled with love from all those who matter to me."— Aly

Amara and Aly | San Francisco, CA | 2023

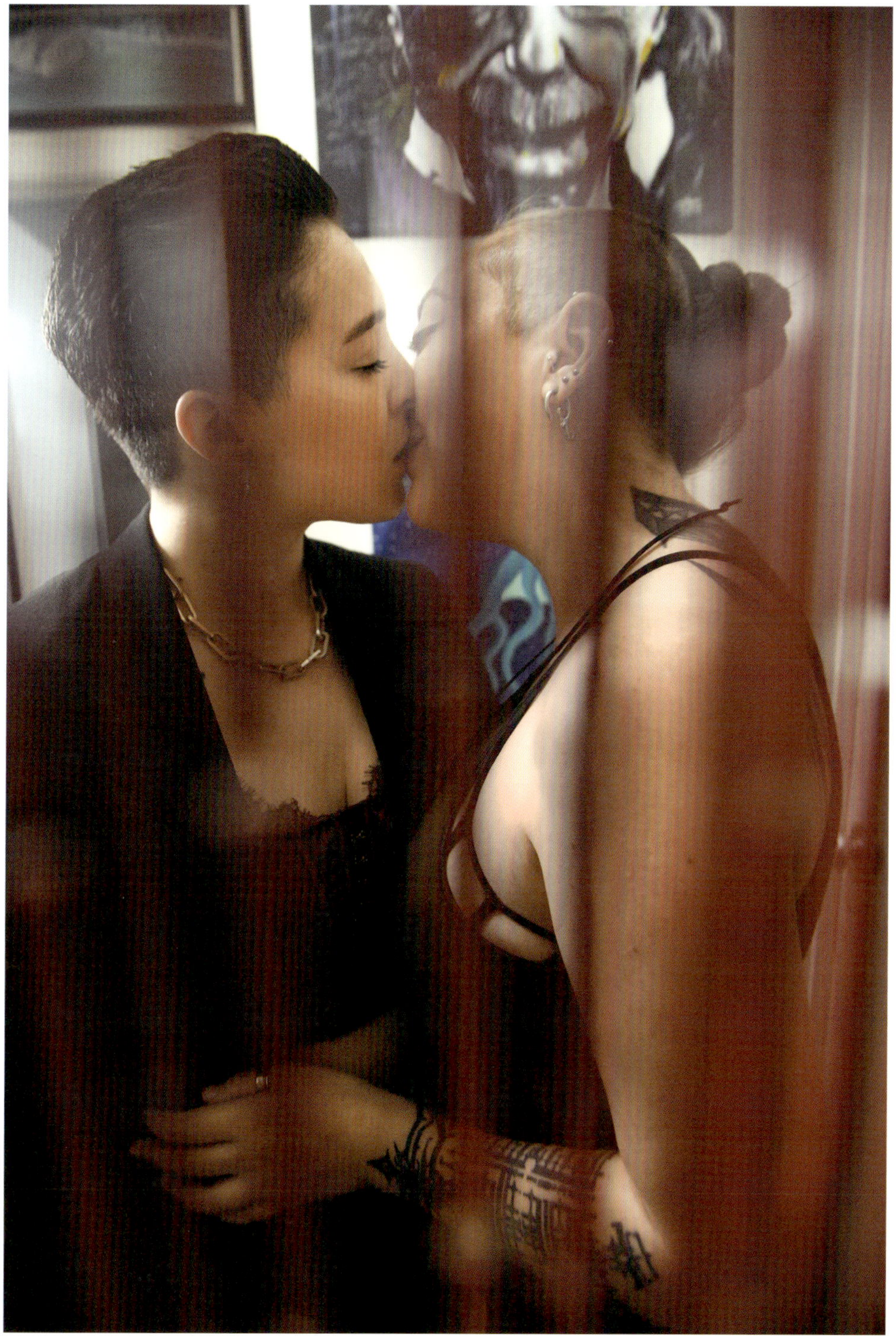

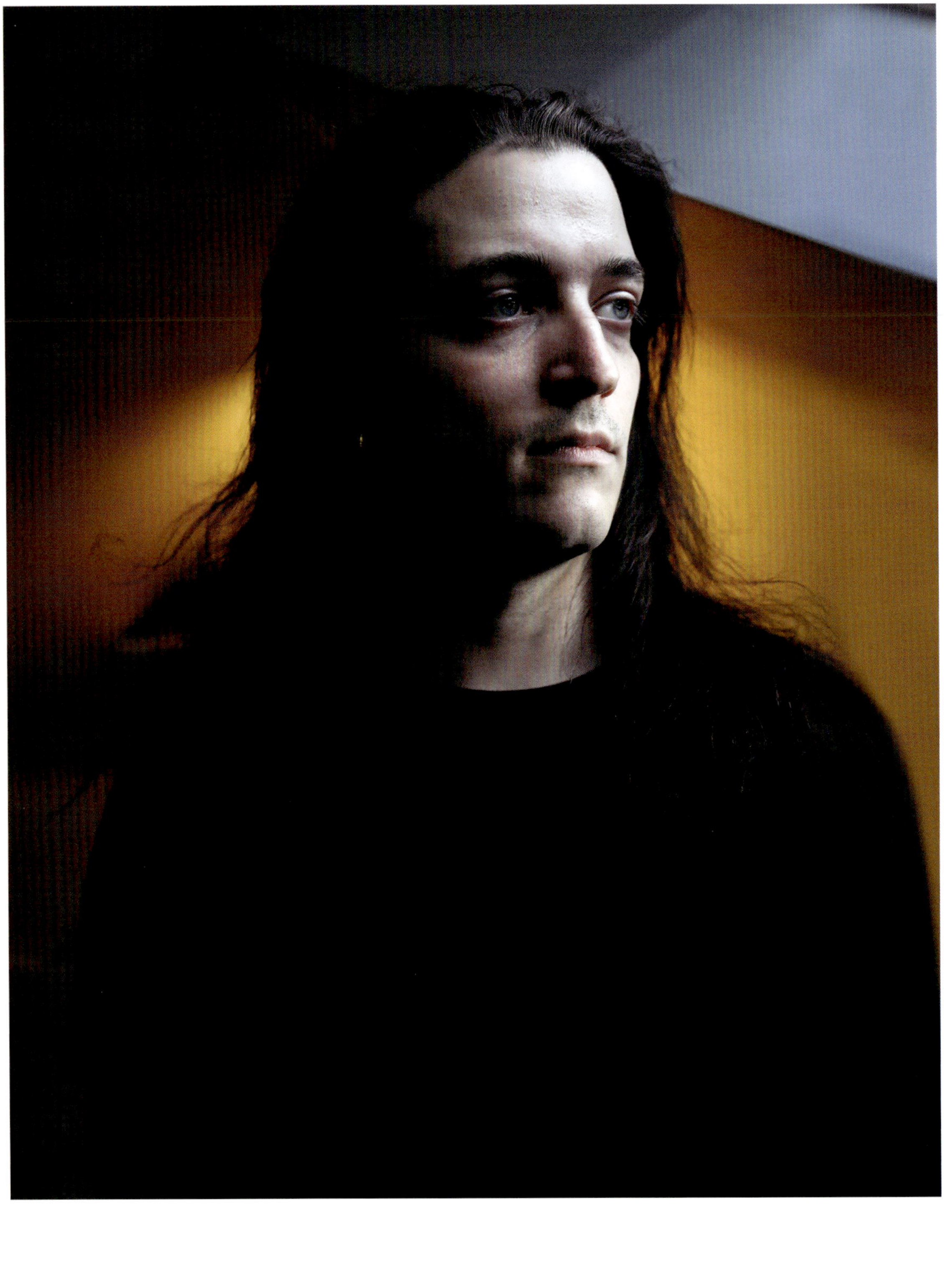

David Iñiguez | Reykjavík, Iceland | 2023

Rodrigo | San Francisco, CA | 2016

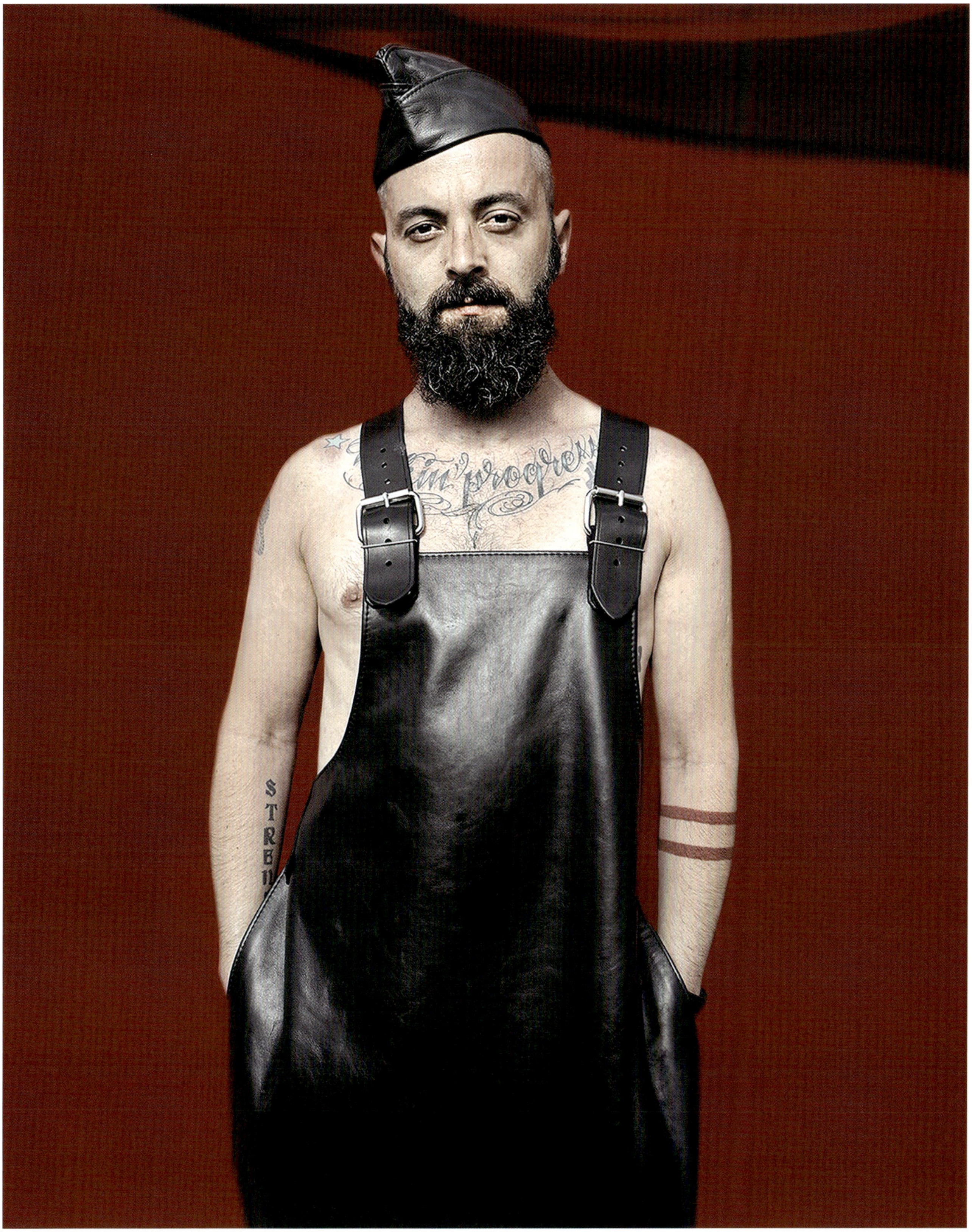

Jeffrey and Amelea | San Francisco, CA | 2016

"Watching a segment on TV on 'Gay Christians,' that single event gave me 'license' to explore my deep-rooted same-sex feelings. I shared with my then wife that I believed I was gay. Ultimately I left the marriage."—Jeffrey

Amelea, Jeffrey's daughter, is also gay. She discovered in middle school that she liked wearing men's clothes and was attracted to girls. "I'm completely fine with my daughter's sexual orientation."—Jeffrey

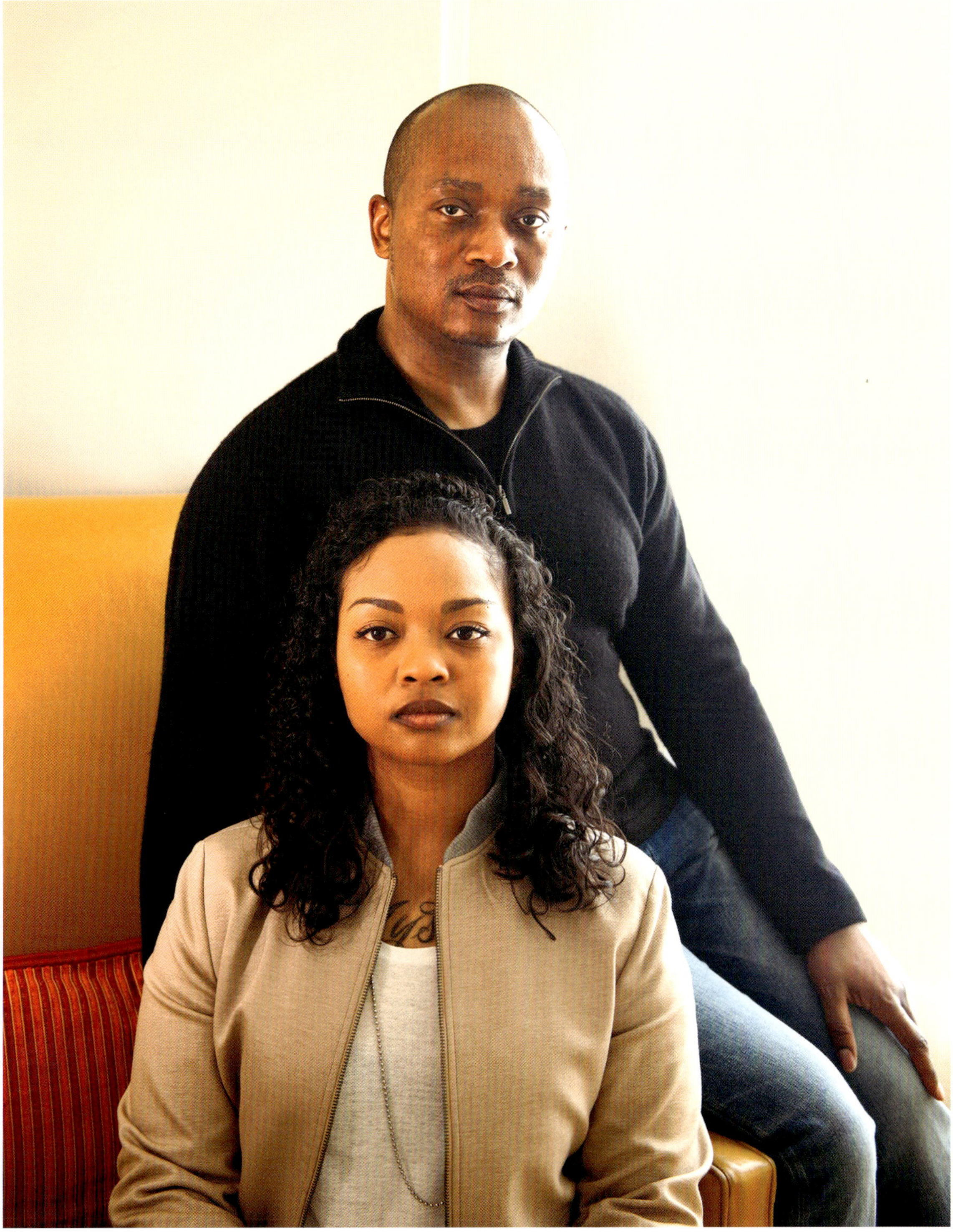

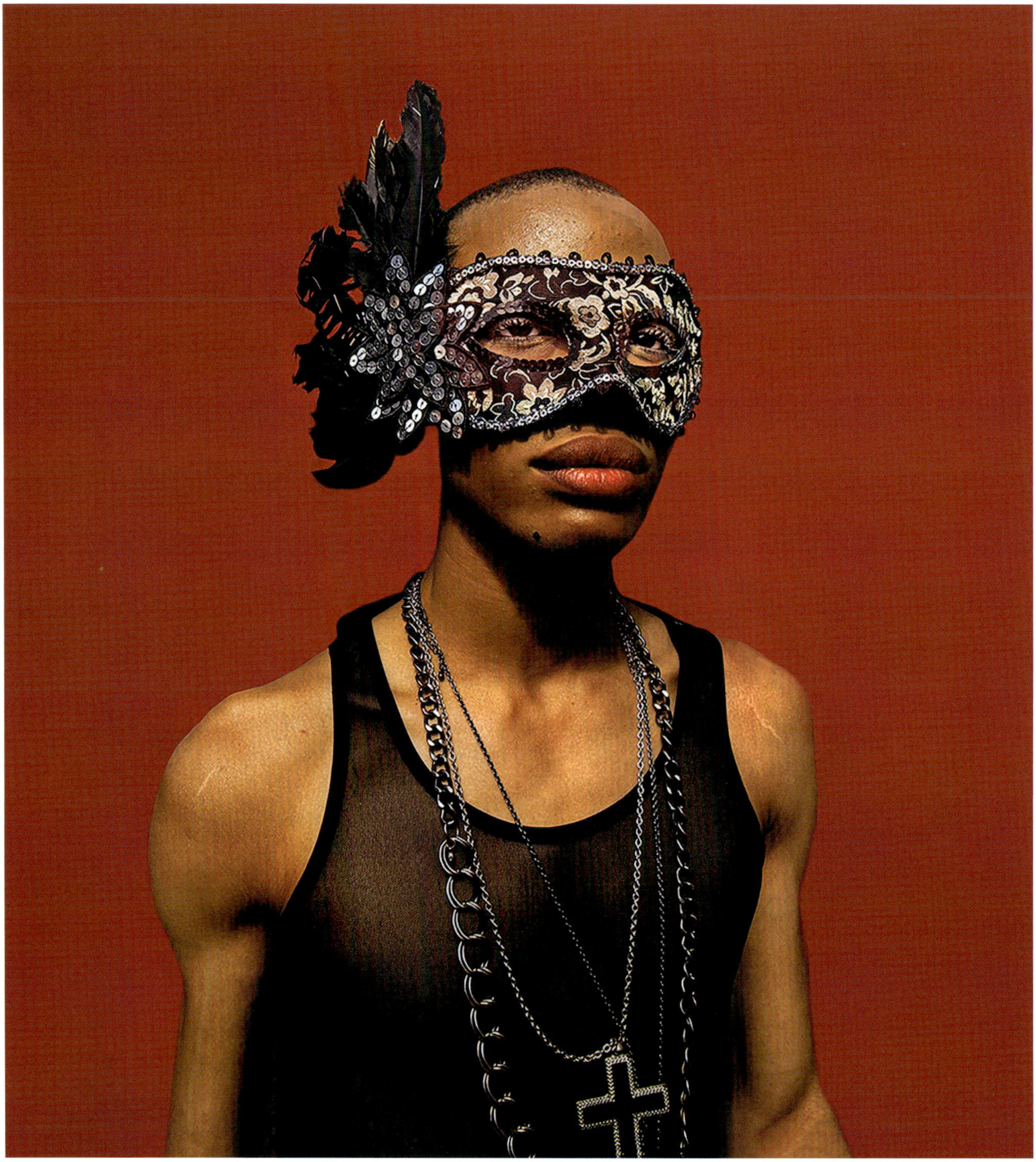

Masquerade | San Francisco, CA | 2018

Brett, Sarah, and Harvey
Oakland, CA | 2017

"My chosen family is a source of unyielding support and encouragement that has given me the freedom to be my authentic self."—Brett

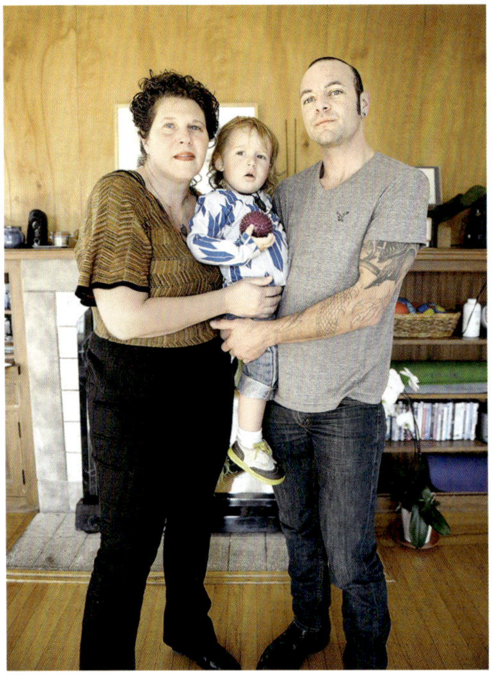

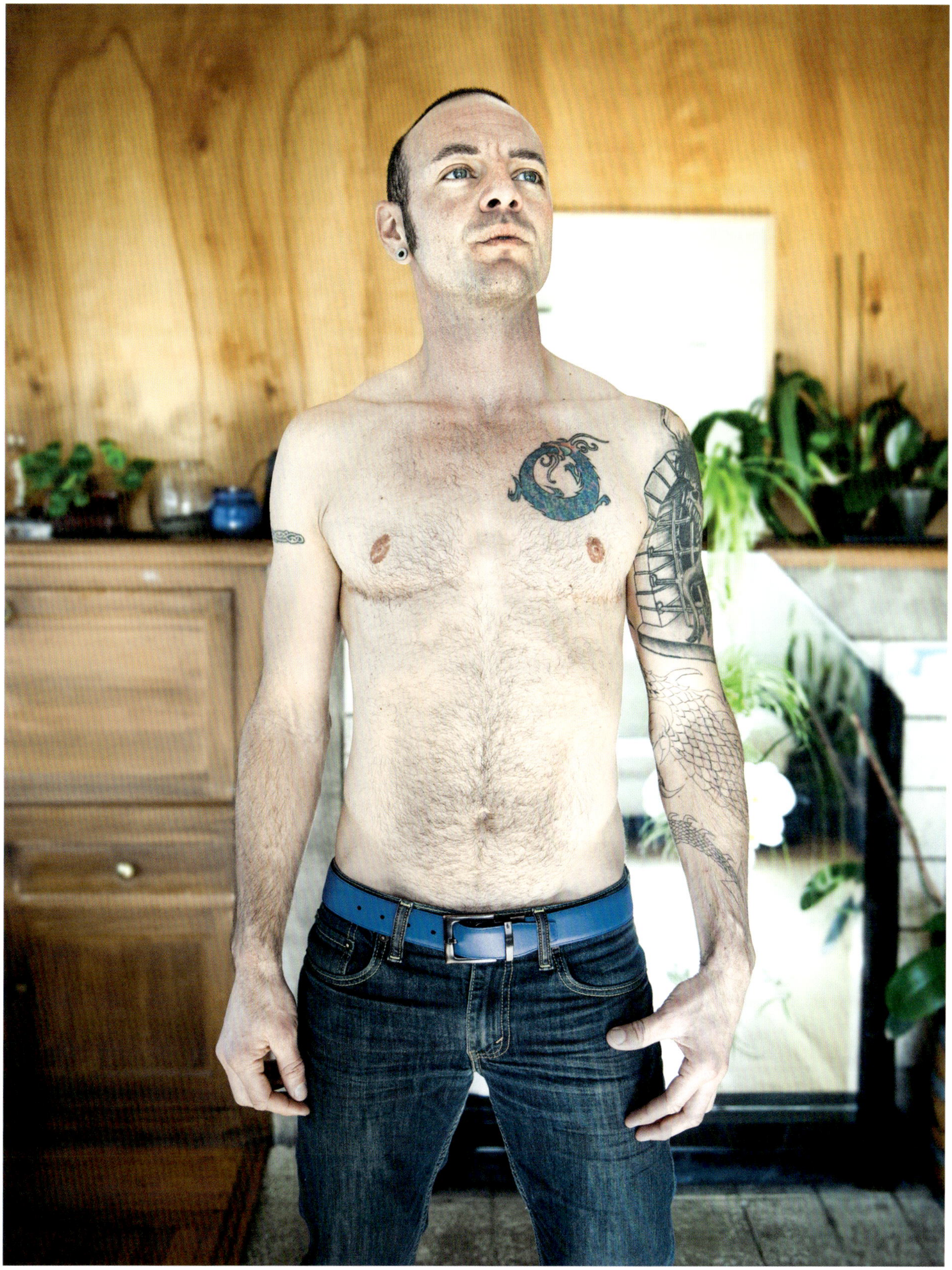

Ariel | San Francisco, CA | 2023

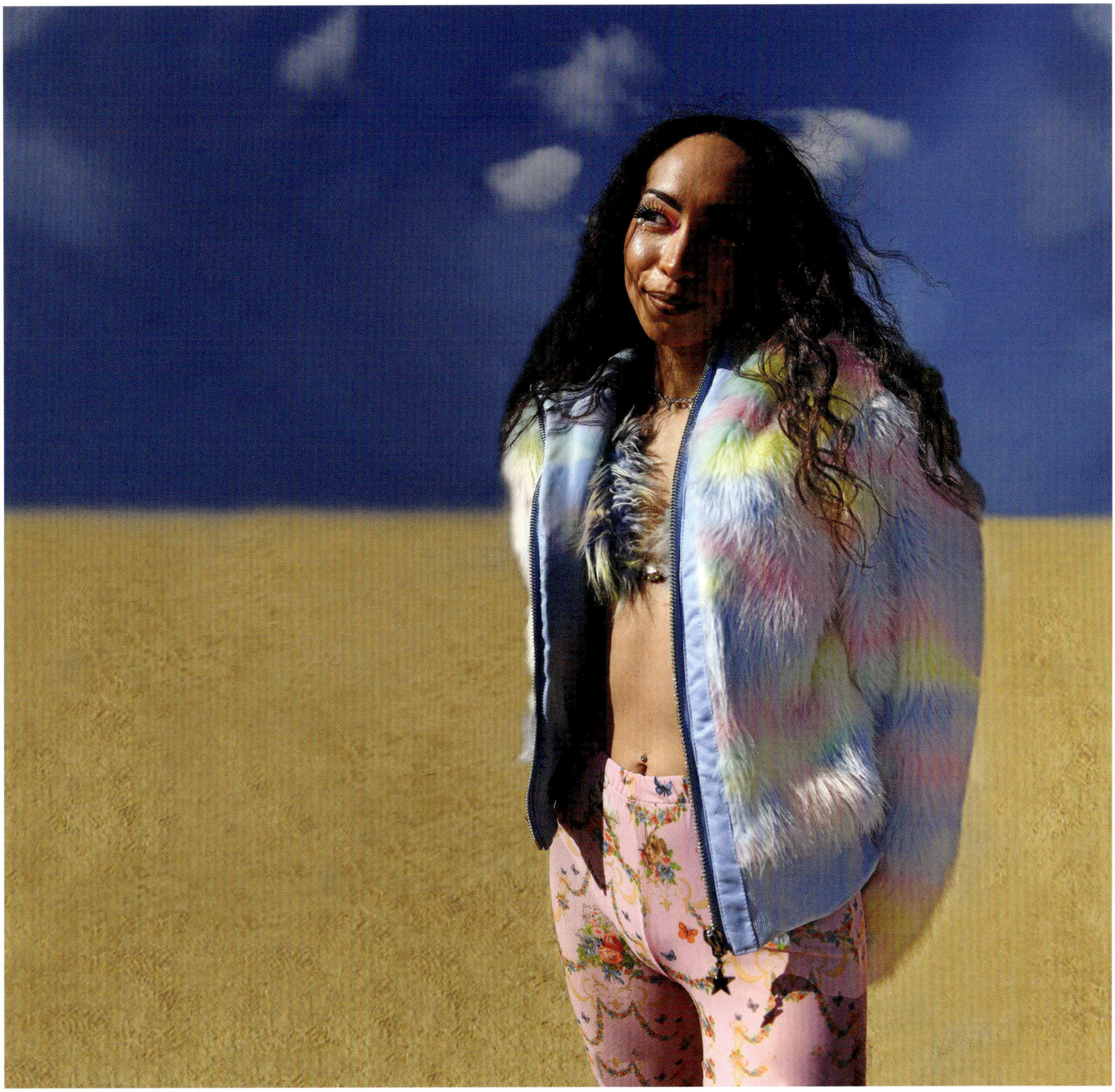

On Folsom Street | San Francisco, CA | 2017

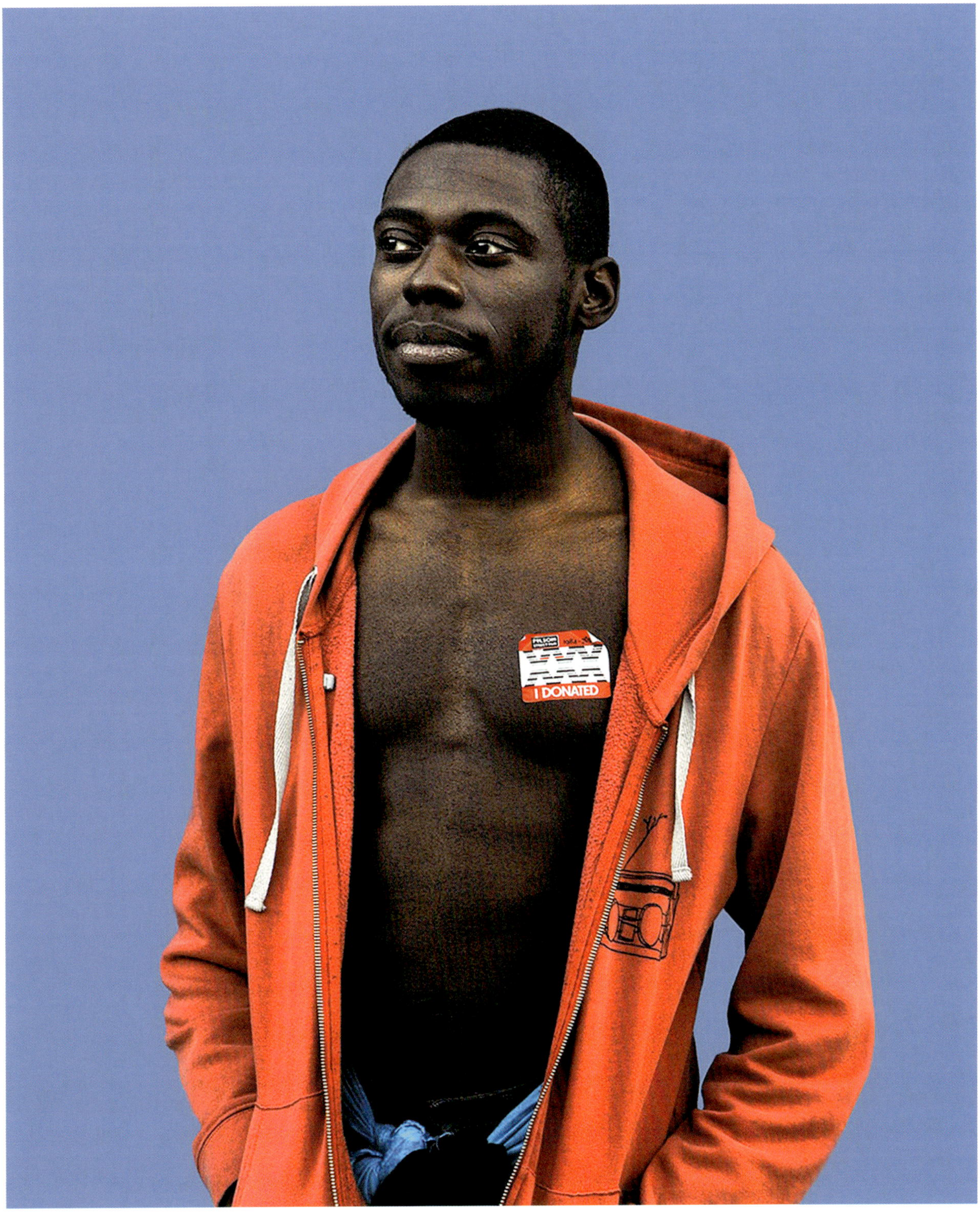
I DONATED

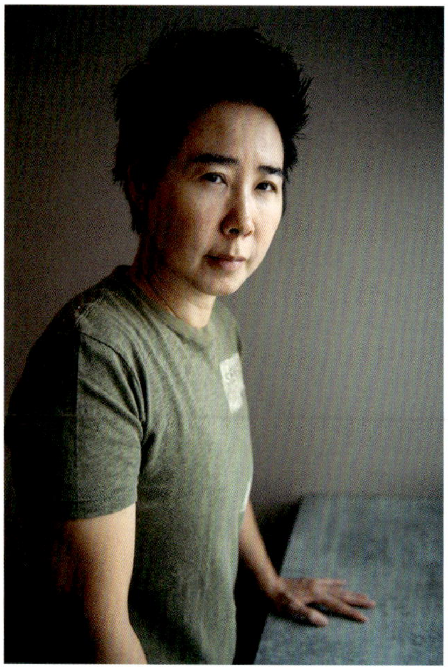

For my mother, Vivian

如果沒有她，我的故事就毫無特別之處
如果沒有她，我相信我仍然困在自我認同的深淵中

如果沒有她，我永遠都無法接受自己

47年前，她賦予我生命
但是
我徬徨
我無助
我封閉
我厭惡自己

31年前
她為我的人生重新上色
在崎嶇難行的人生路上為我披荊斬棘
我們手牽手打造了一座堅固的城堡
從此之後
城堡內漸漸絢麗多彩、百花齊放
—葦薇

Without her, my story would be nothing special.
Without her, I believe I would still be stuck in the abyss of self-identity

I could never accept myself without her

Forty-seven years ago, she gave me life
But
I'm hesitant
I'm helpless
I'm closed
I hate myself

Thirty-one years ago, she recolored my life
Overcoming obstacles for me on the rugged road of life
Hand in hand we build a strong castle
henceforth
The castle gradually becomes more colorful and flowers bloom.
—Wei, Wei

Wei Wei and Vivian
Taipei, Taiwan | 2023

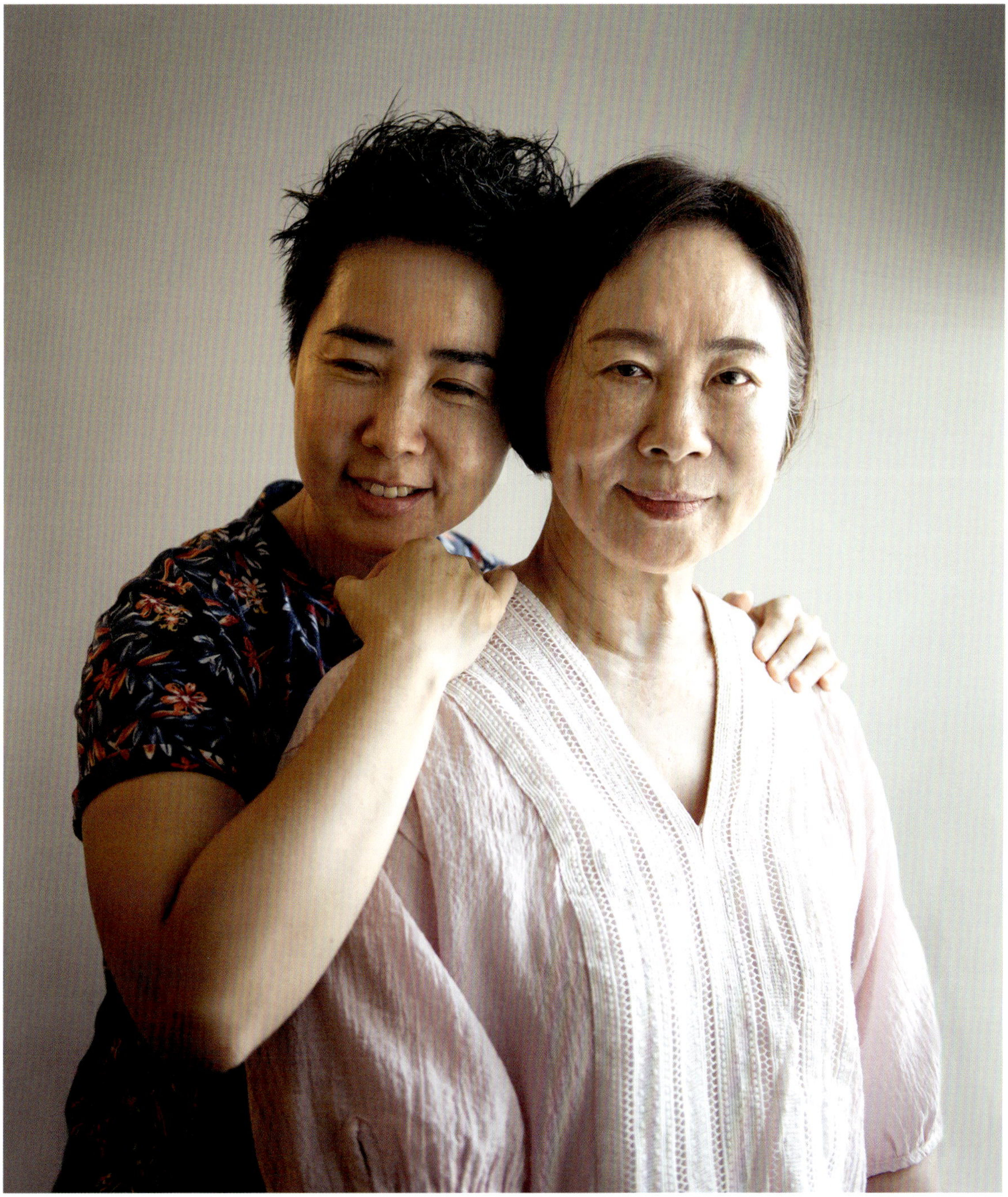

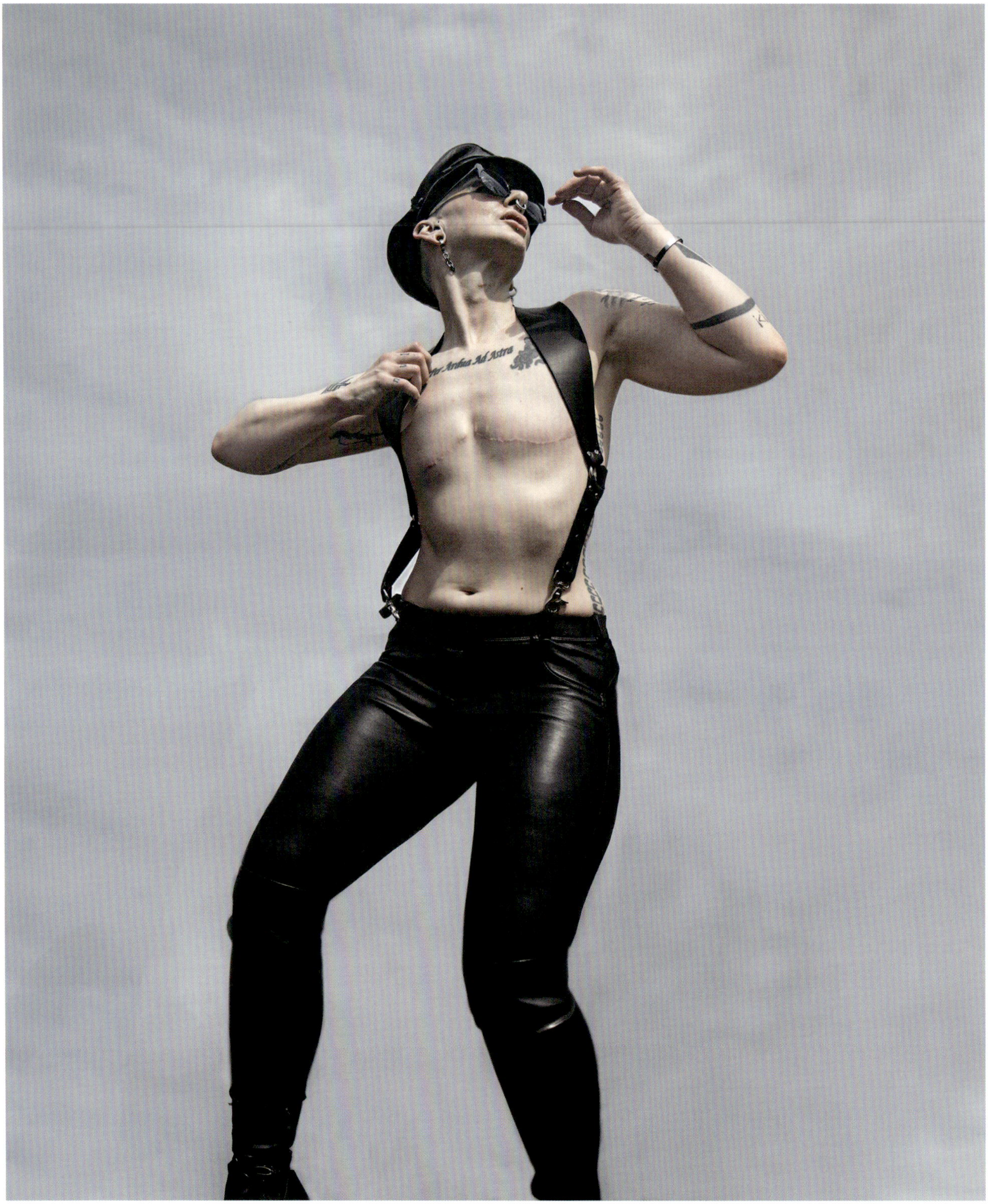

Lori | San Francisco, CA | 2020

Barbara and Jess

San Francisco, CA | 2023

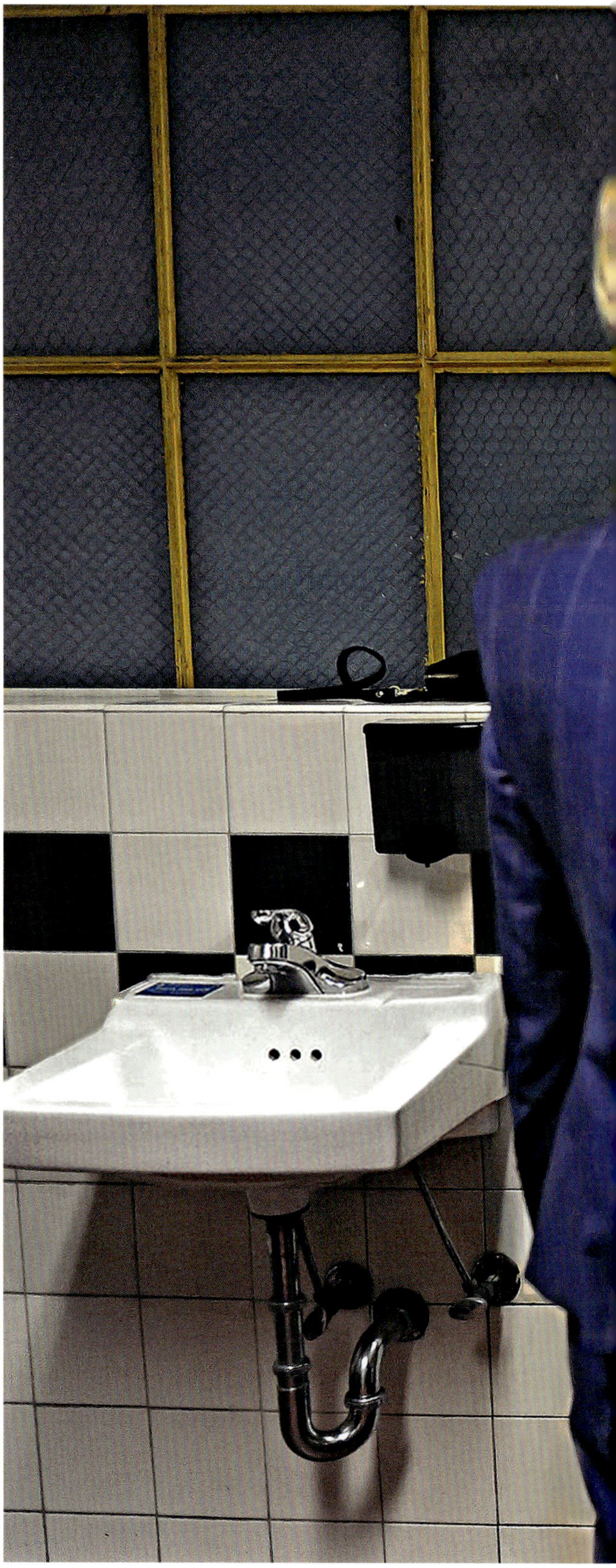

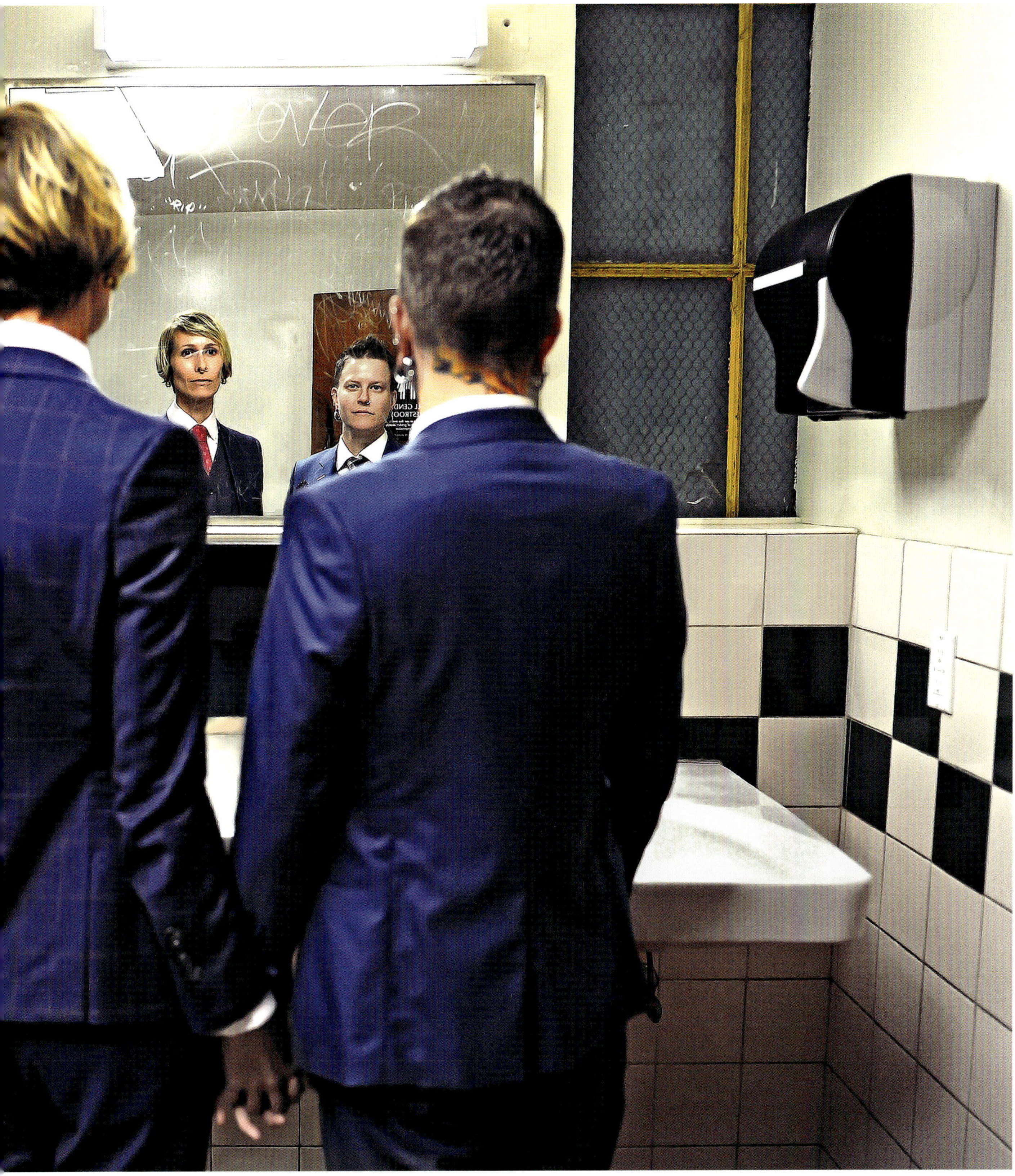

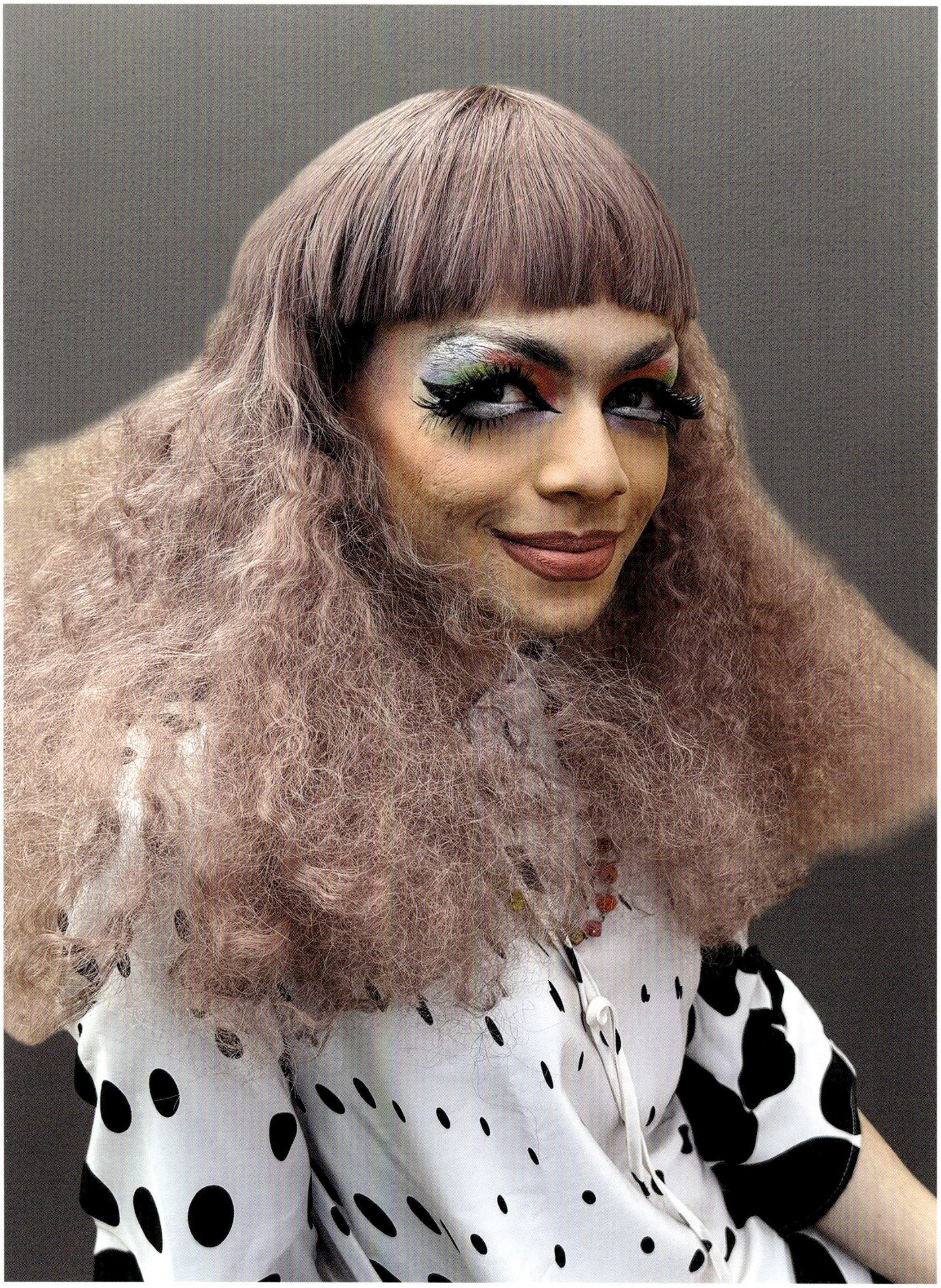

Jenny | San Francisco, CA | 2023

Hot Love | San Francisco, CA | 2018

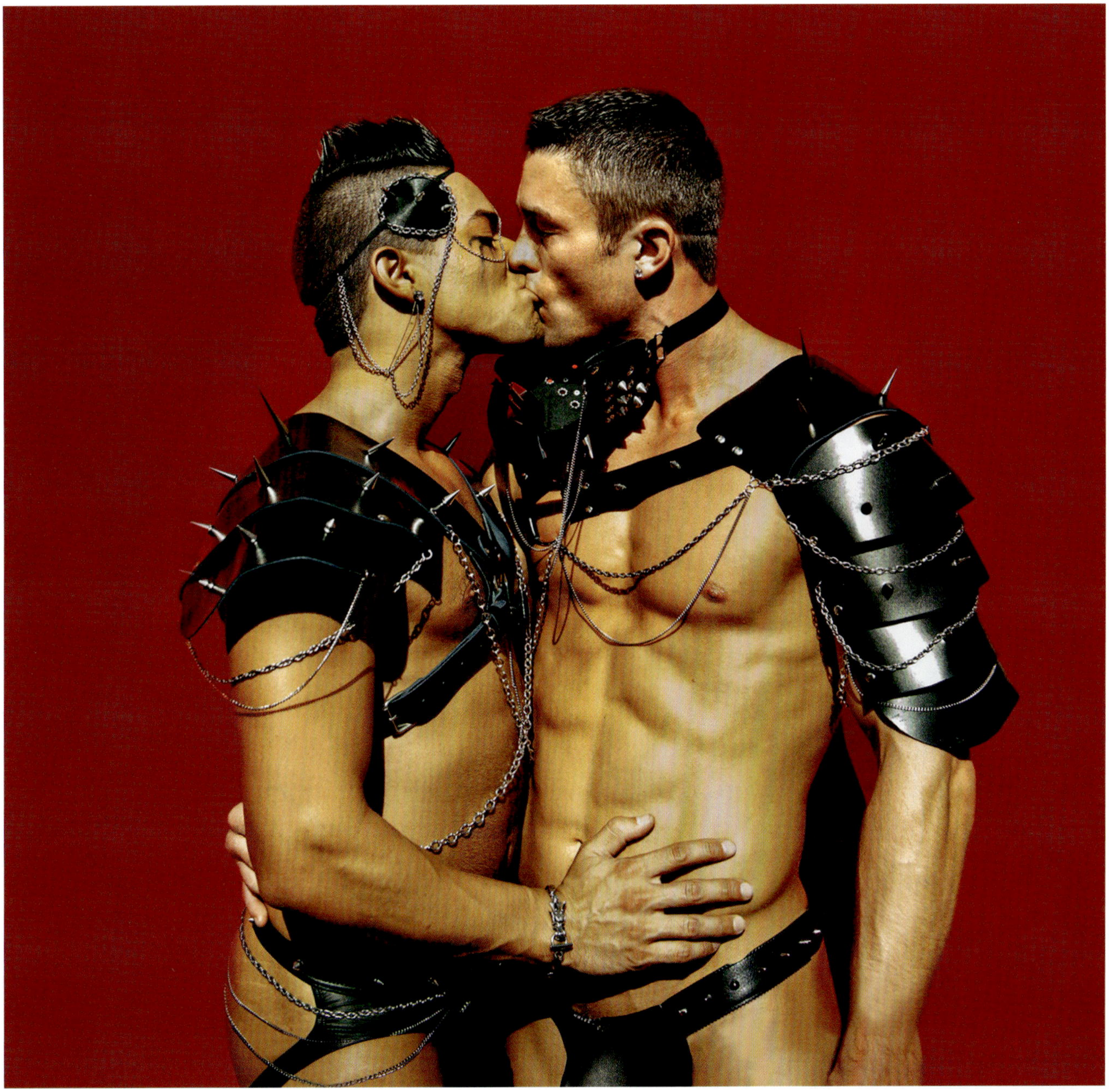

Camille | San Francisco, CA | 2023

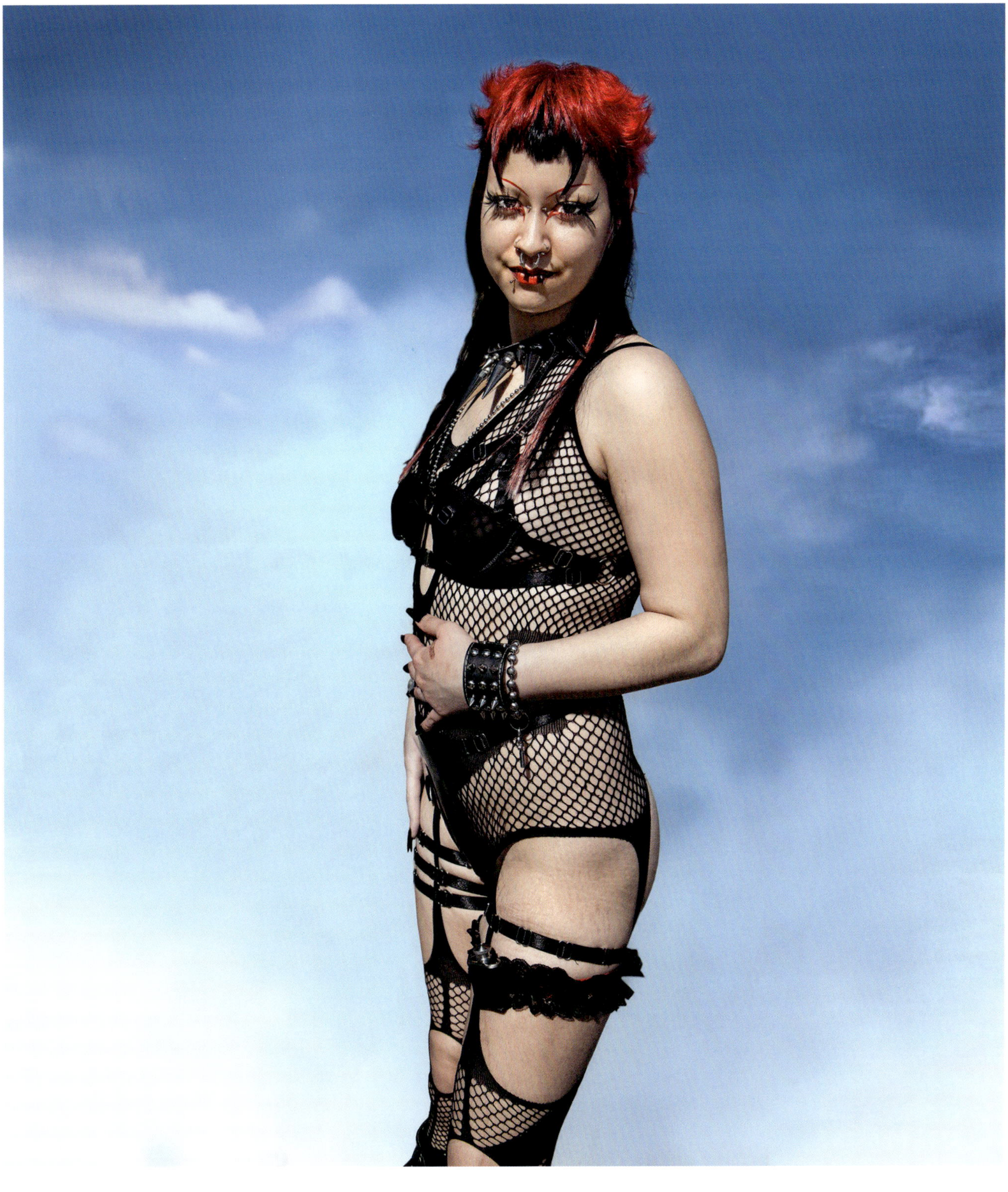

Metamorphosis | Woodland, CA | 2019

I met Thai, an aerialist, at a charity event in San Francisco. I asked him about his passion and how he identifies with this unique profession. He described himself as someone in a state of metamorphosis as he takes to the air, spinning and tumbling through highs and lows in acrobatic maneuvers, experiencing a kind of transcendence and rebirth that gives him deep and powerful freedom, change and hope.

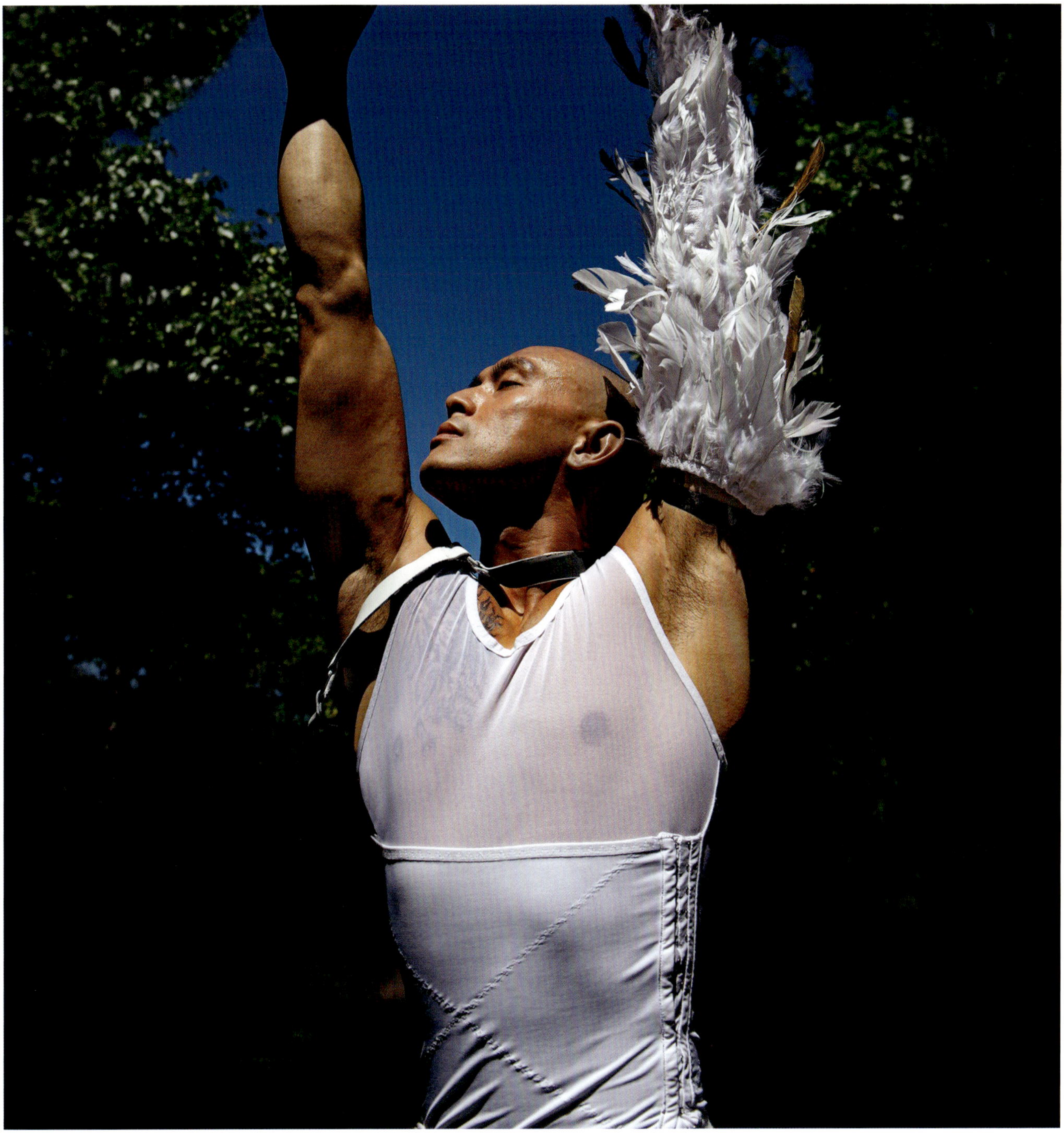

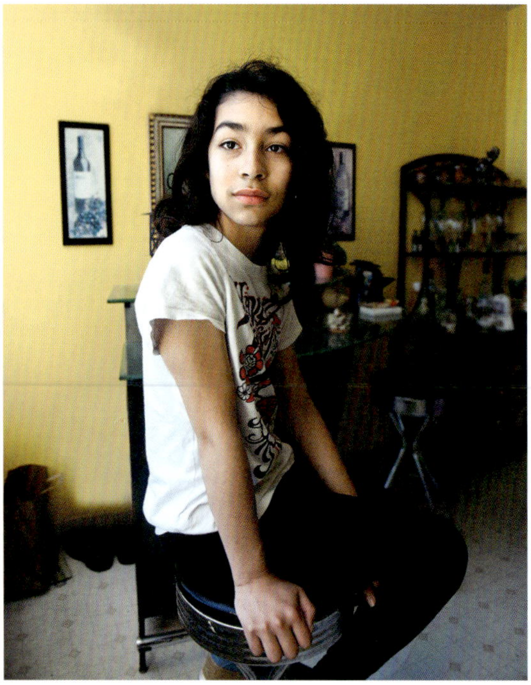

Alexis and Irma | San Mateo, CA | 2017

"I liked to play dolls and dressing up ever since I was three. Growing up with my parents' difficult relationship was hard. They got divorced. My mom is a strong woman and raised me, allowing me to be who I want to be."—Alexis

"Alexis is my *only* daughter. I live and breathe for her. She is my whole life and I will help and support her until the end."—Irma

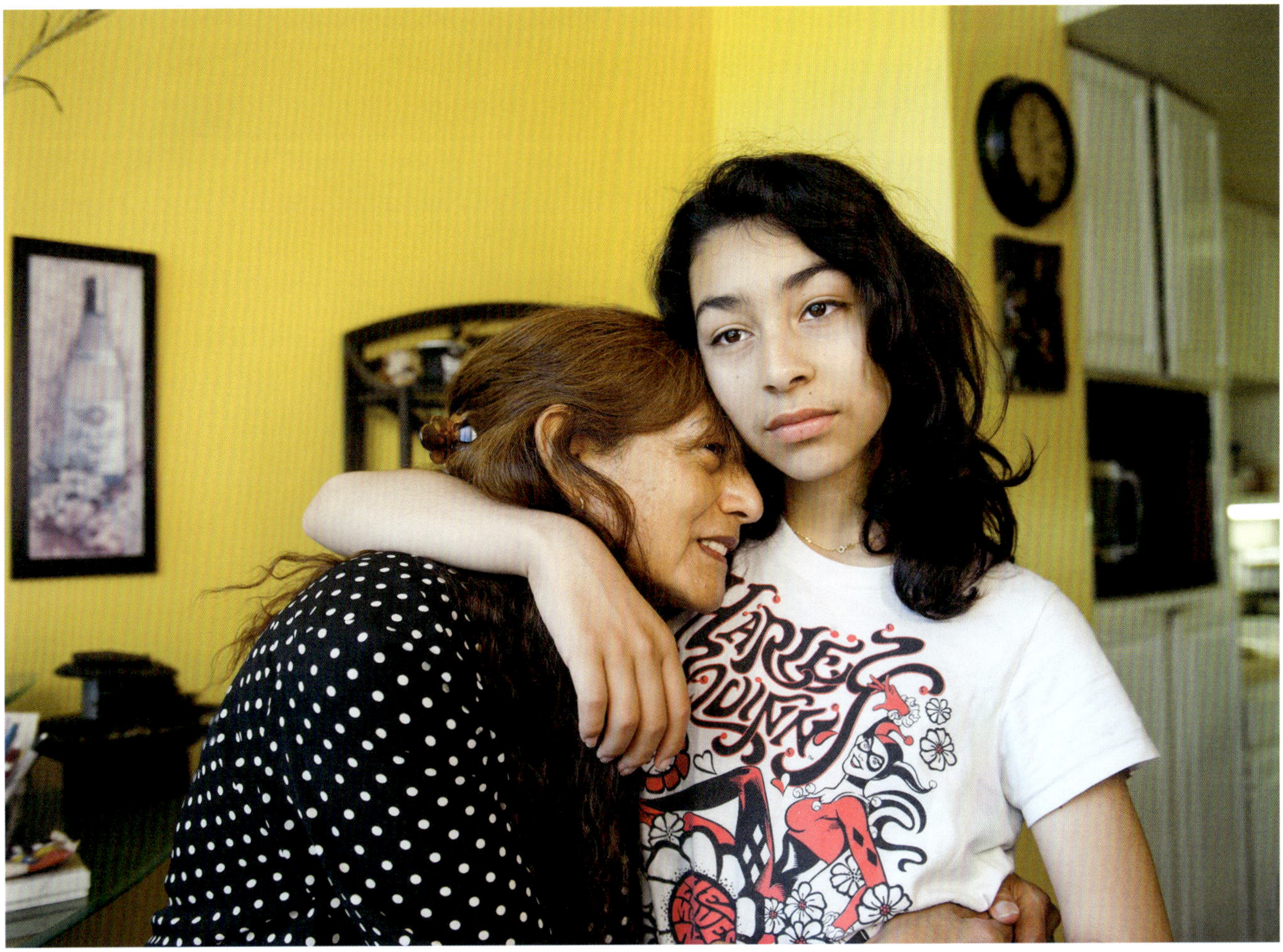

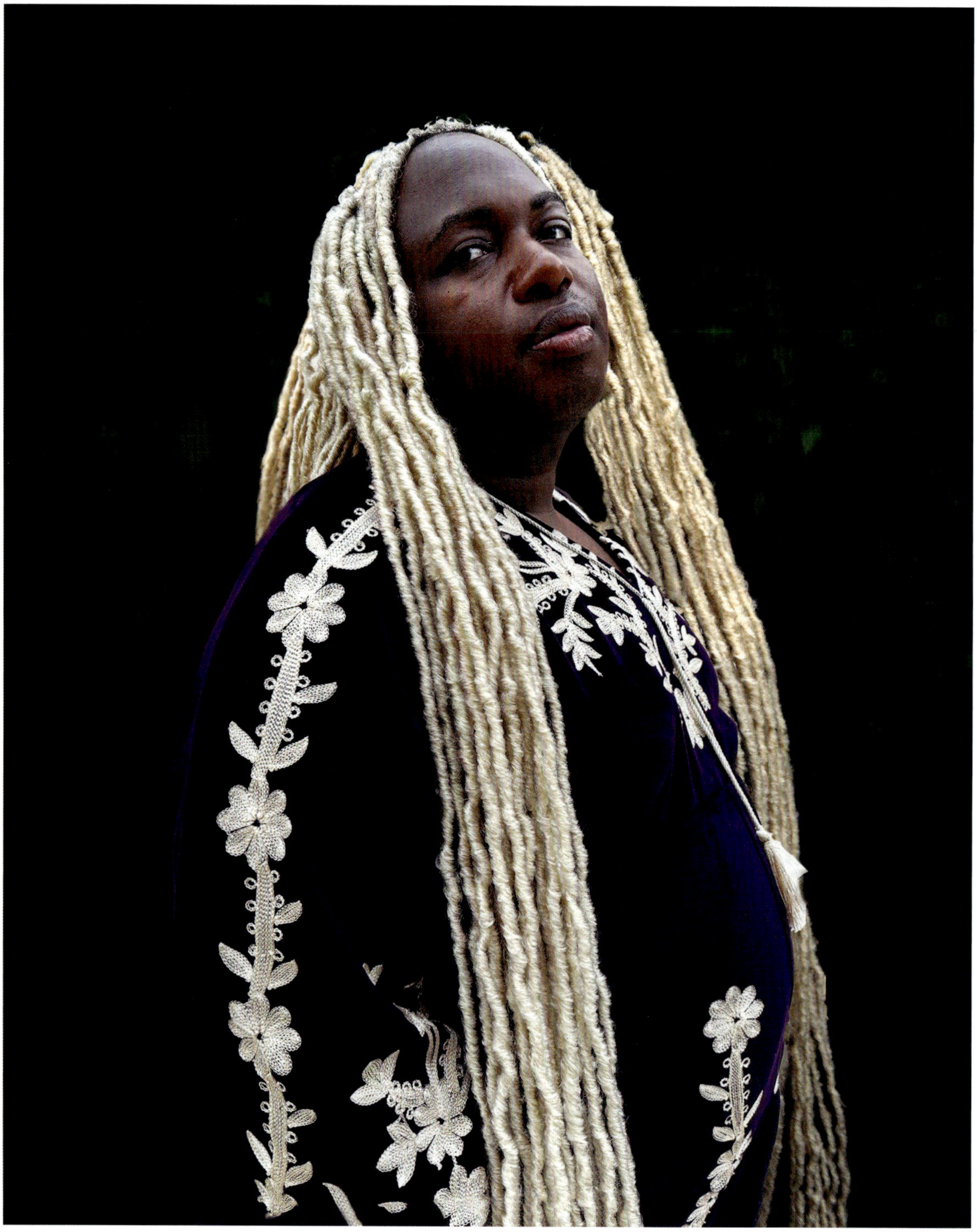

Ceraun the DivaNun | Inglewood, CA | 2023

"My journey to my queerness is less like one of coming out and more like a continuing unfolding. For me the issue was never my desires but the boxes society wanted me to exist in. I've always overflowed my boundaries, whether it was my desire for men or to be seen as something more than a man. Thankfully my family and friends have always been supportive of my transformations. Because in the moment before every unfolding I had to transcend my fear of what they would say in order to put my truth first."
— Ceraun the DivaNun

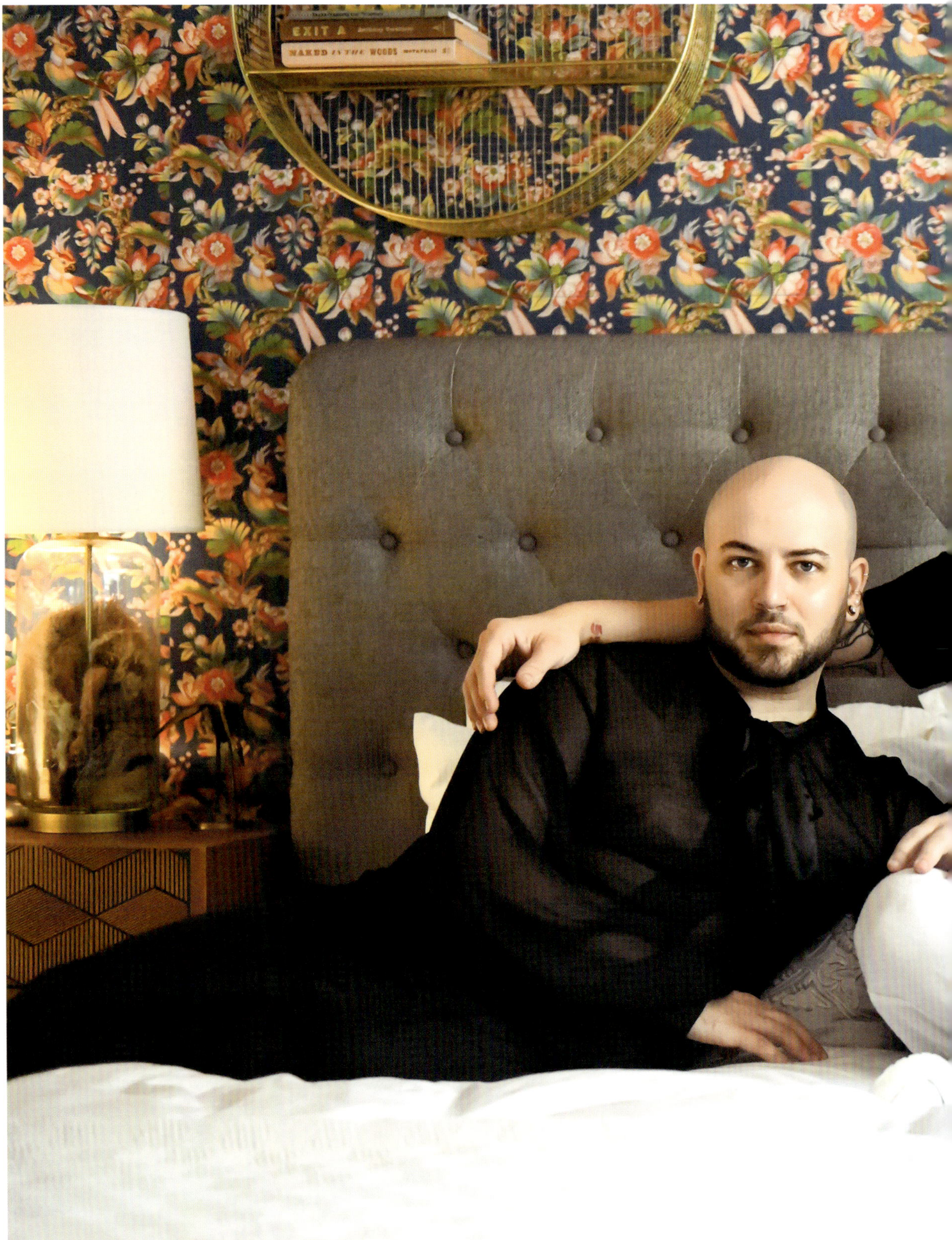

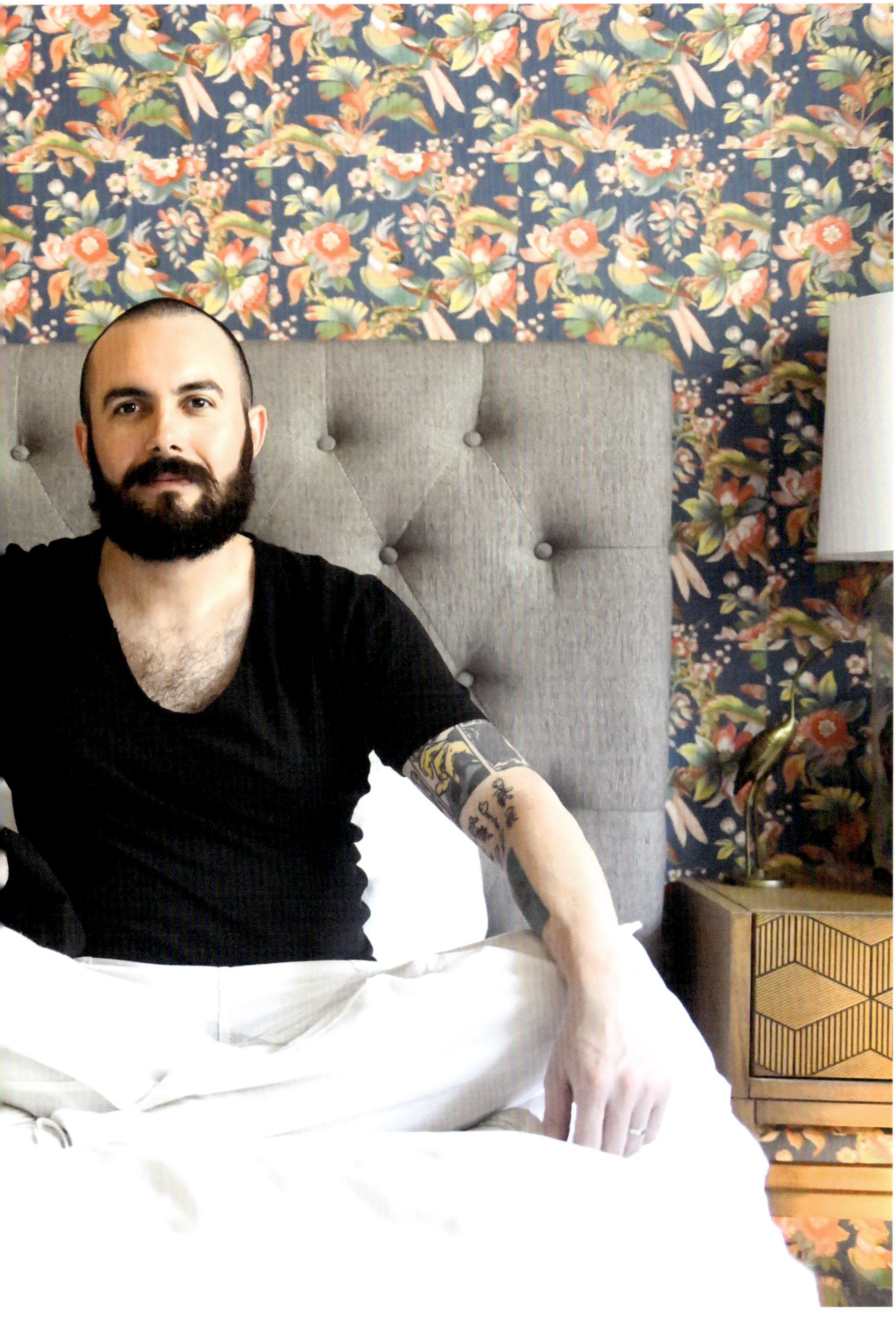

Alex and Alej
Oakland, CA | 2019

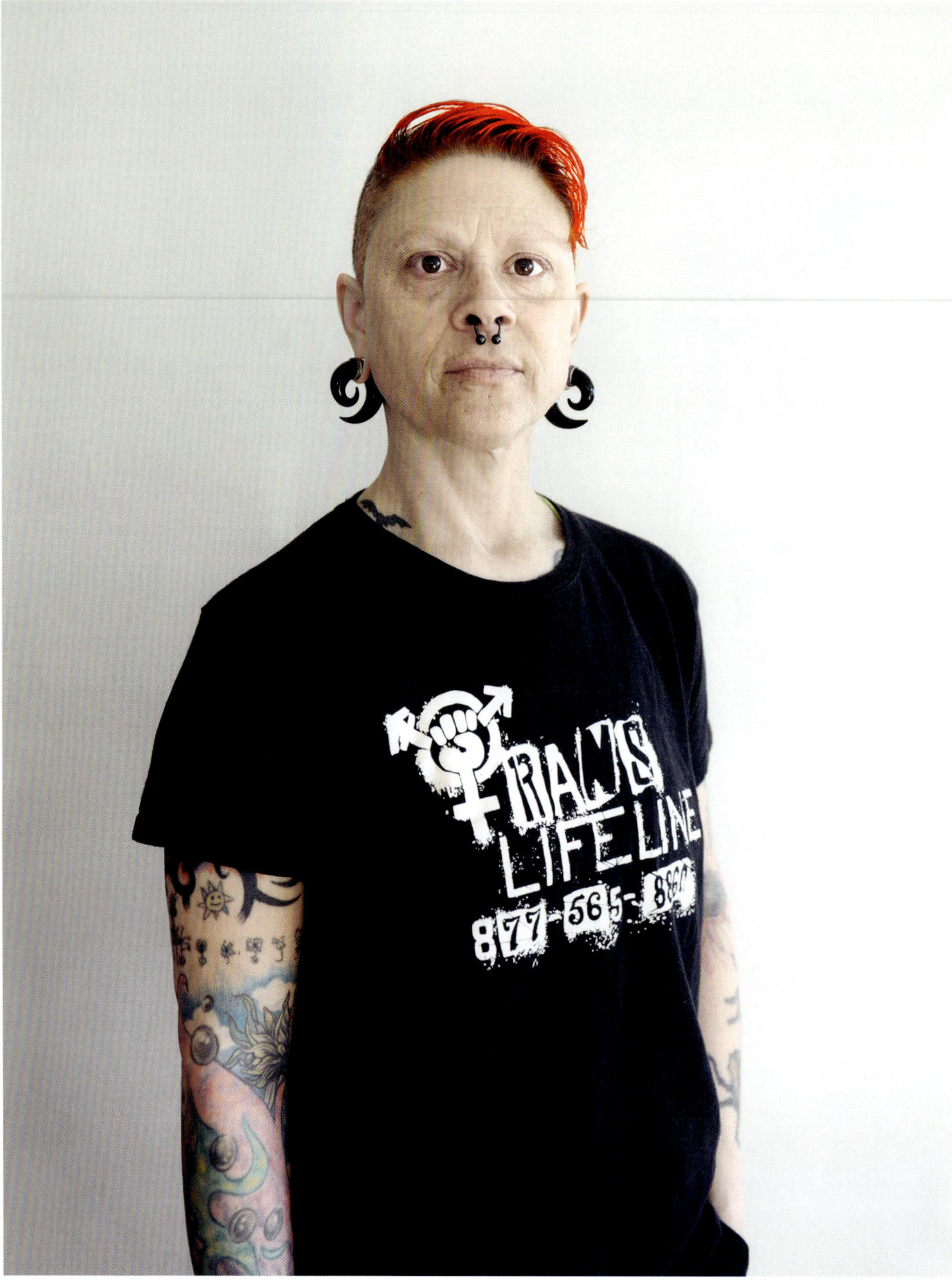
LIFE LINE

Lauren | Oakland, CA | 2017

Megan | San Francisco, CA | 2017

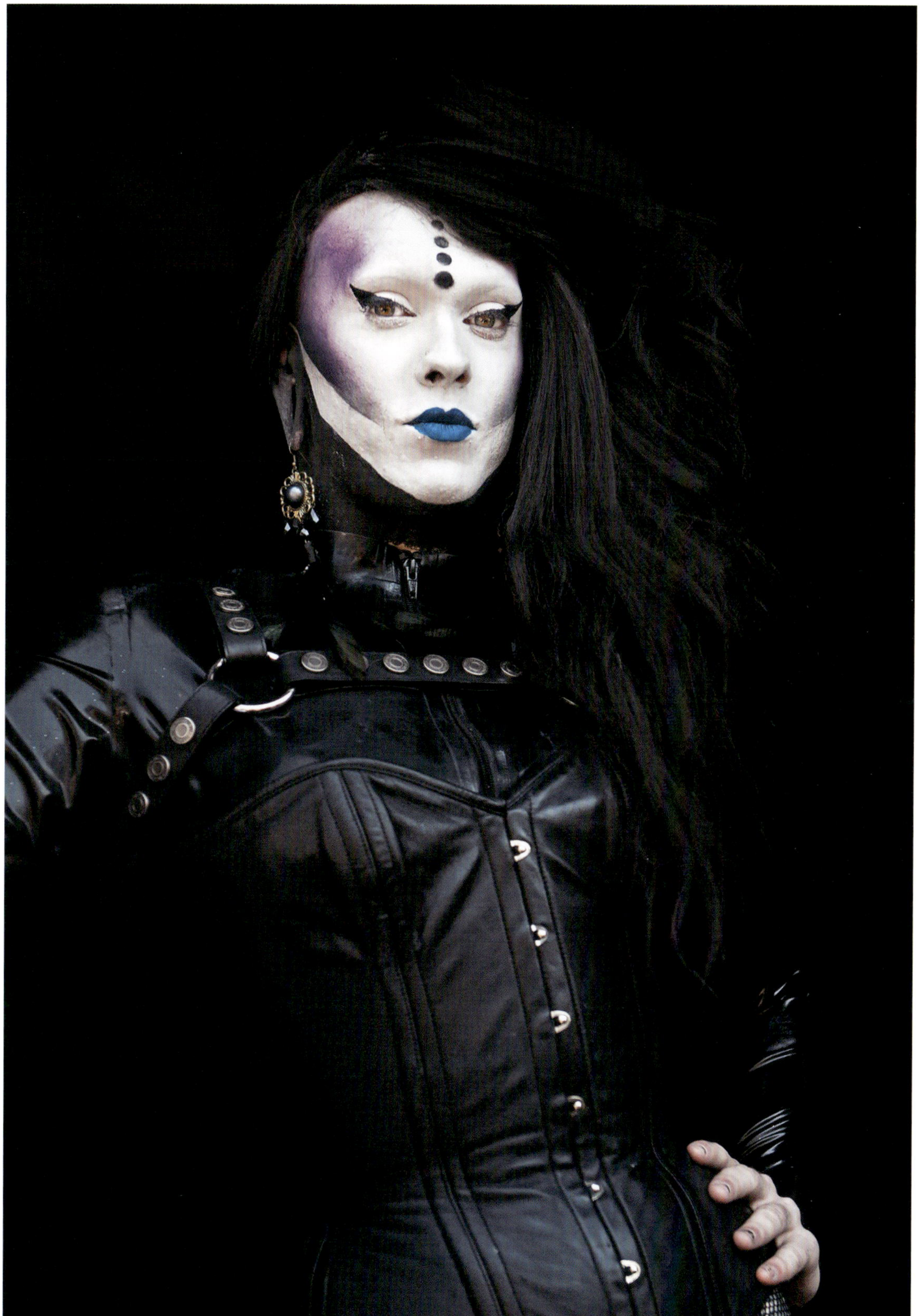

Davey and Daenara | Oakland, CA | 2017

"Her soul in division from itself
Climbing, falling She knew not where,
Her knee-cap broken, that girl I declare
A beautiful lofty thing, or a thing
Heroically lost, heroically found.

No common intelligible sound
But sang, "O sea-starved, hungry sea."
—From "A Crazed Girl" by W. B. Yeats

The poem was tattooed on Davey's body.

I first met Davey at a street fair. They weren't wearing anything on their body. I was intrigued by their demeanor, their beauty and vulnerability. I have come to learn about the tragedy in their tragic life. They were neglected by their mother, raped by a babysitter at age six and then a gang of kids in grade school. Davey developed multi-personalities as a result of childhood traumas.

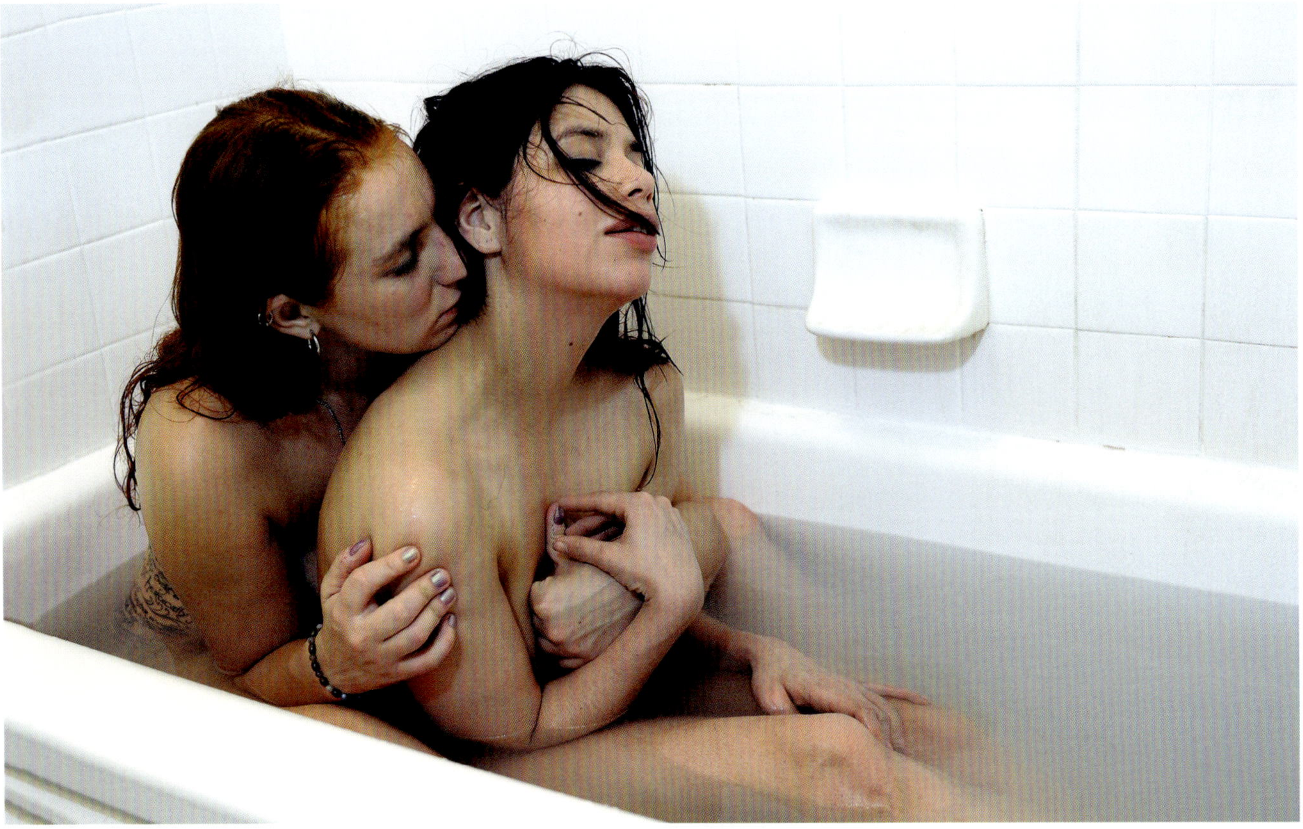

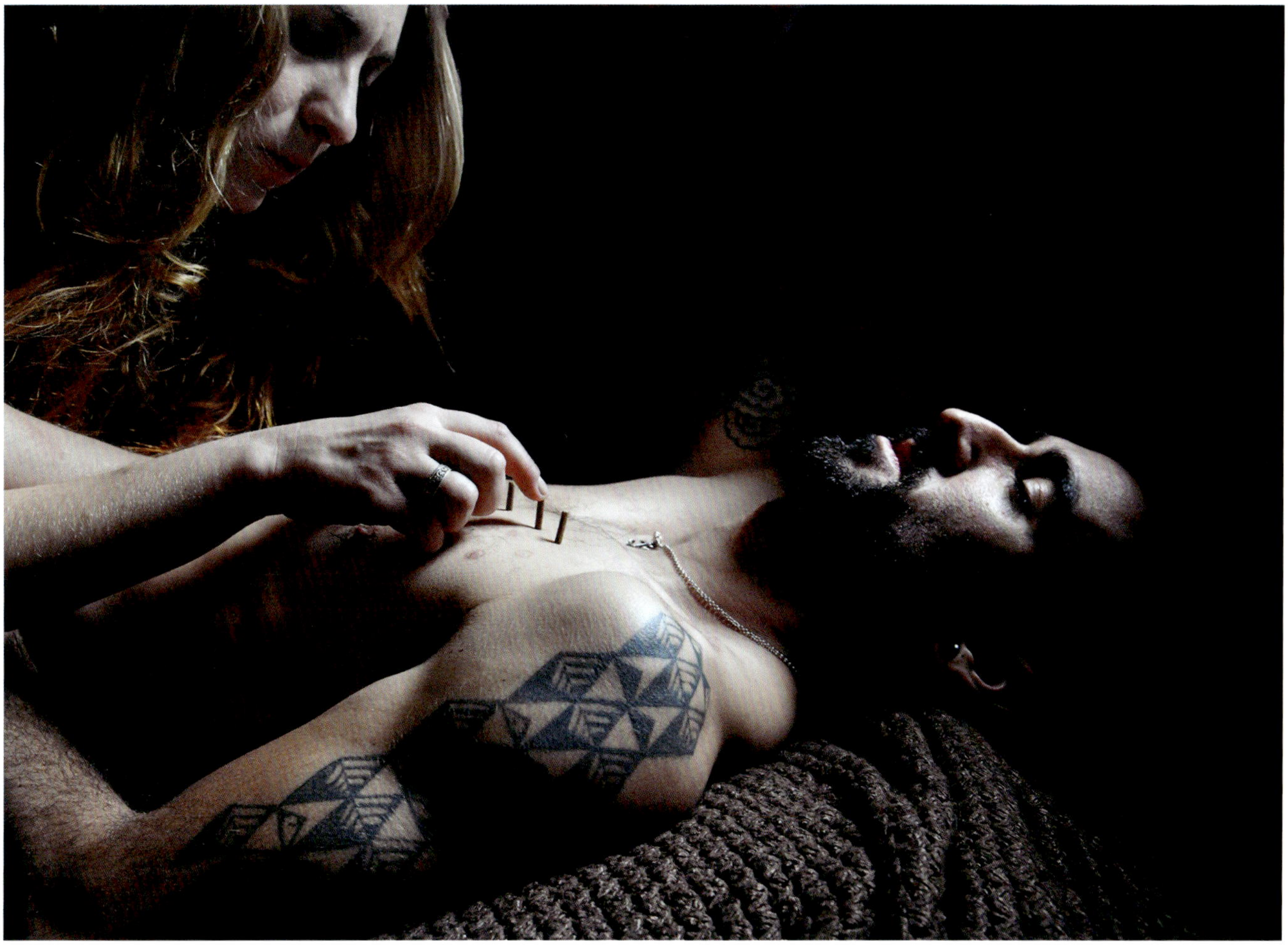

Davey and Allan (right)

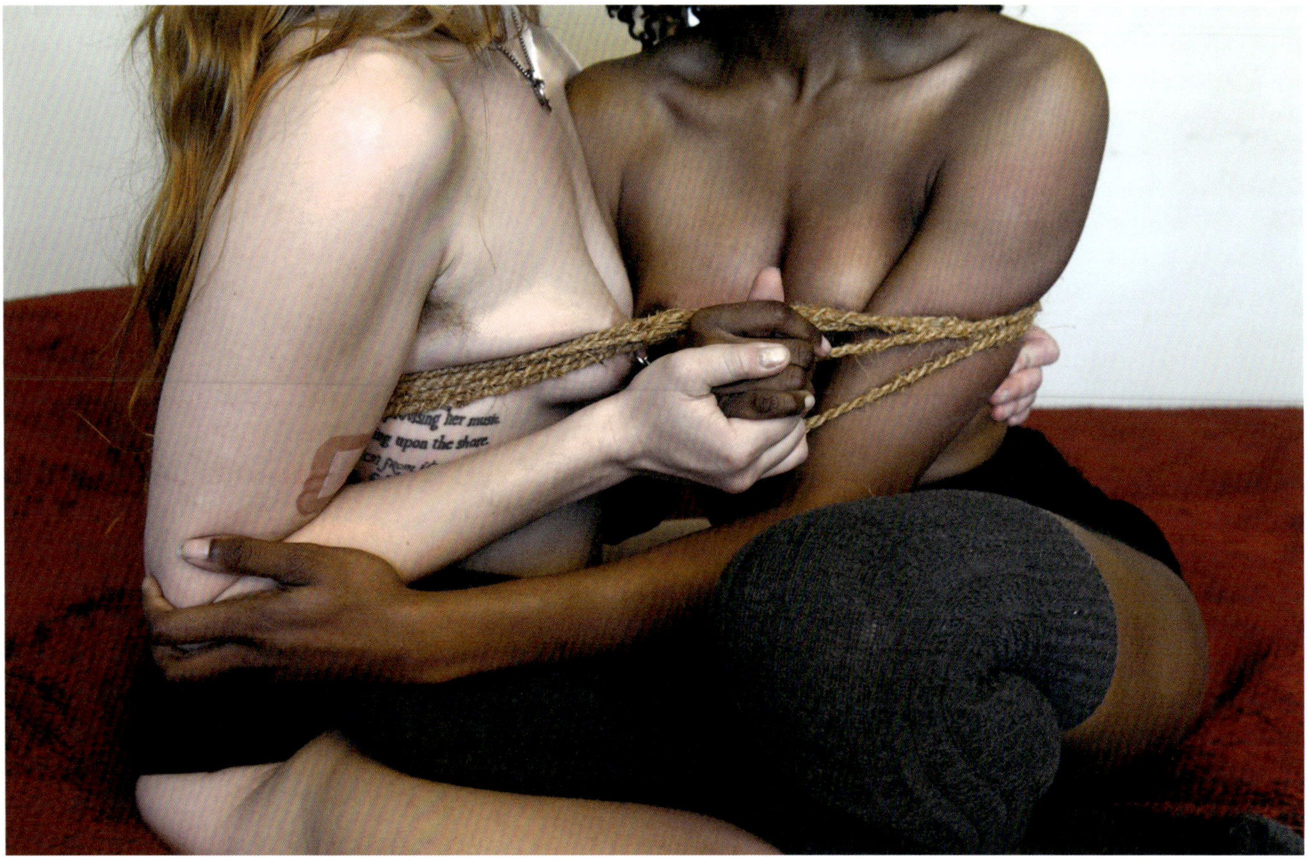

Davey and Ari | Oakland, CA | 2017

Davey has worked as a writing assistant, babysitter, but mostly a BDSM rope performer. Their emotional world is complex and constantly finds balance in daily life from love through polyamorous relationships with multiple partners, such as Bridger Daenara, Allan, Ari, and others. For Davey, the freedom and the ability to explore more amorphic forms of connection and expressions of love than what normative society prescribes is "how you are supposed to connect." Davey and their partners embrace sex positivity and celebrate the full gender spectrum. As Davey says, "They are *all* important, even if every individual relationship is custom-designed."

Davey | San Francisco, CA | 2016

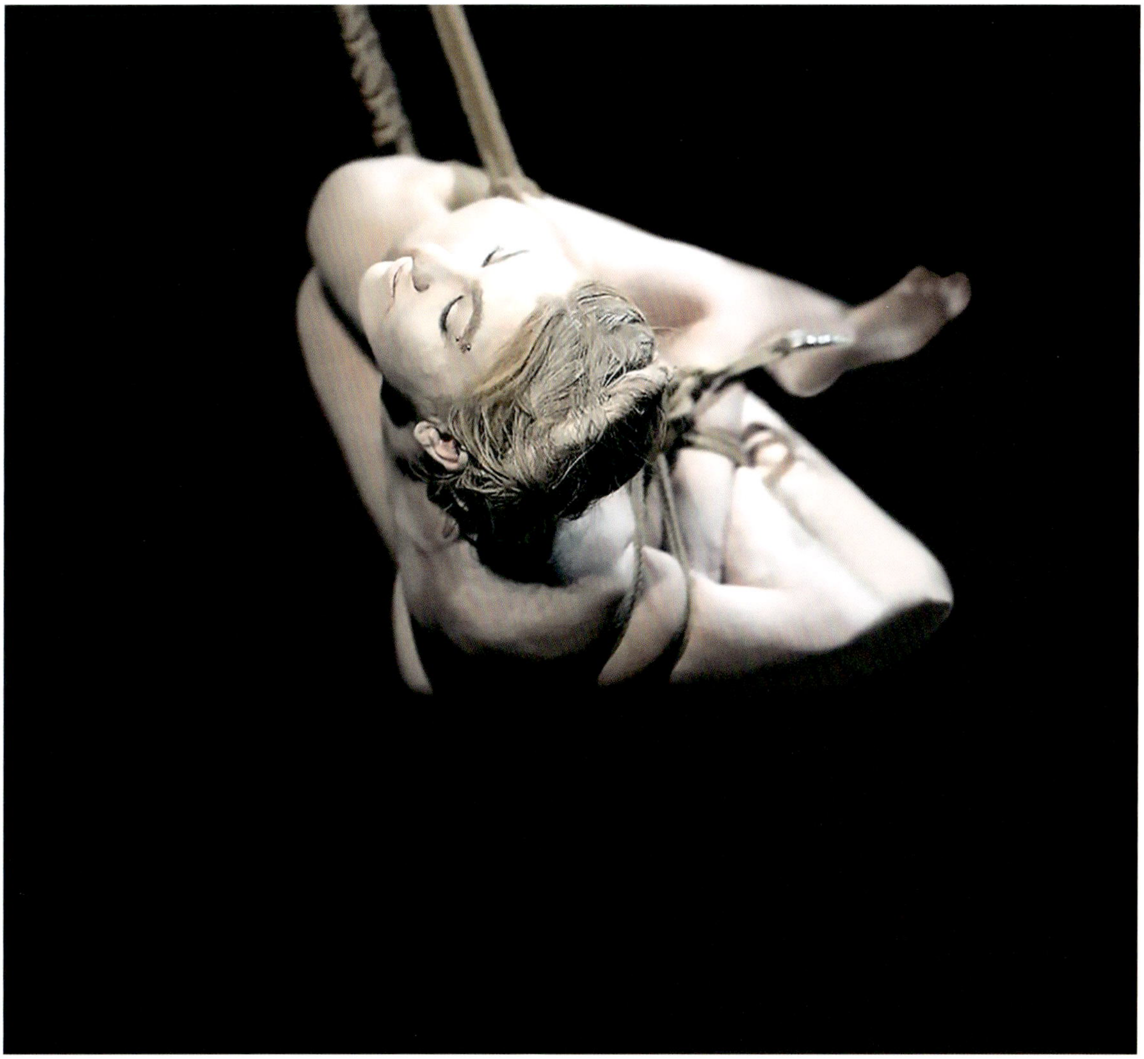

Flower People | Castro, CA | 2022

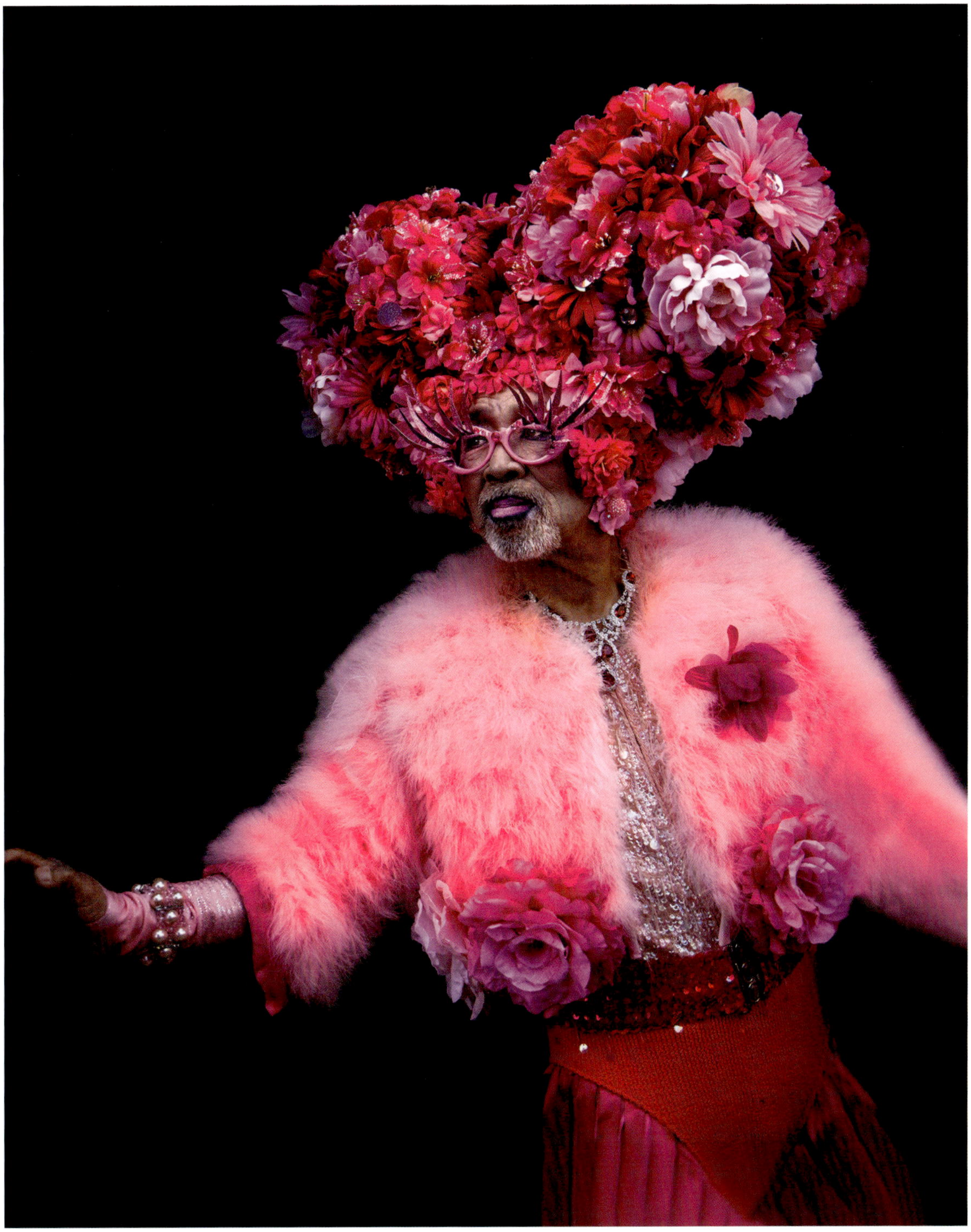

Hiroki and Desun
San Francisco, CA | 2020

"My name is Hiroki. I'm 29 years old and I'm genderqueer. Twenty-five was a transformational time in my life. I was on testosterone and I was coming into my chosen name: Hiroki, which means joy and strength. My grandmother passed away around this time, so many things were in flux for me.

It was also around this time that I started to heal around my religious trauma. My dad uses his religion as justification for disowning me as both a queer and trans person. This is why healing around my spirituality is really important for me. Healing religious trauma was directly connected to coming out as trans because when I started to accept my gender identity, I started to accept all of me, which included being a spiritual person.

Realizing I was trans changed the trajectory of my life. Living my trans truth has taught me so much about compassion, kindness, and patience, first with myself and then with others.

Desun and I met in 2014 in an Asian American studies class at San Francisco State University. Desun is one of my best friends and it was such a joy to see him in the Bay Area. Our friendship grew when we lived in DC in the winter of 2016–2017. He is one of the first people I could really practice boundaries with and have conversations about my needs and energy levels and how I struggle with codependency. This is one of the most healing friendships I've ever been a part of. I learn so much from our friendship. And he's just so damn funny! Desun is one of my chosen family and I am beyond grateful for their wisdom, care, and compassion. They teach me tenderness and how to unpack masculinity as masculine people of color. I feel seen and held by them. And being loved by them has taught me new possibilities about masculinity and healing as a survivor."

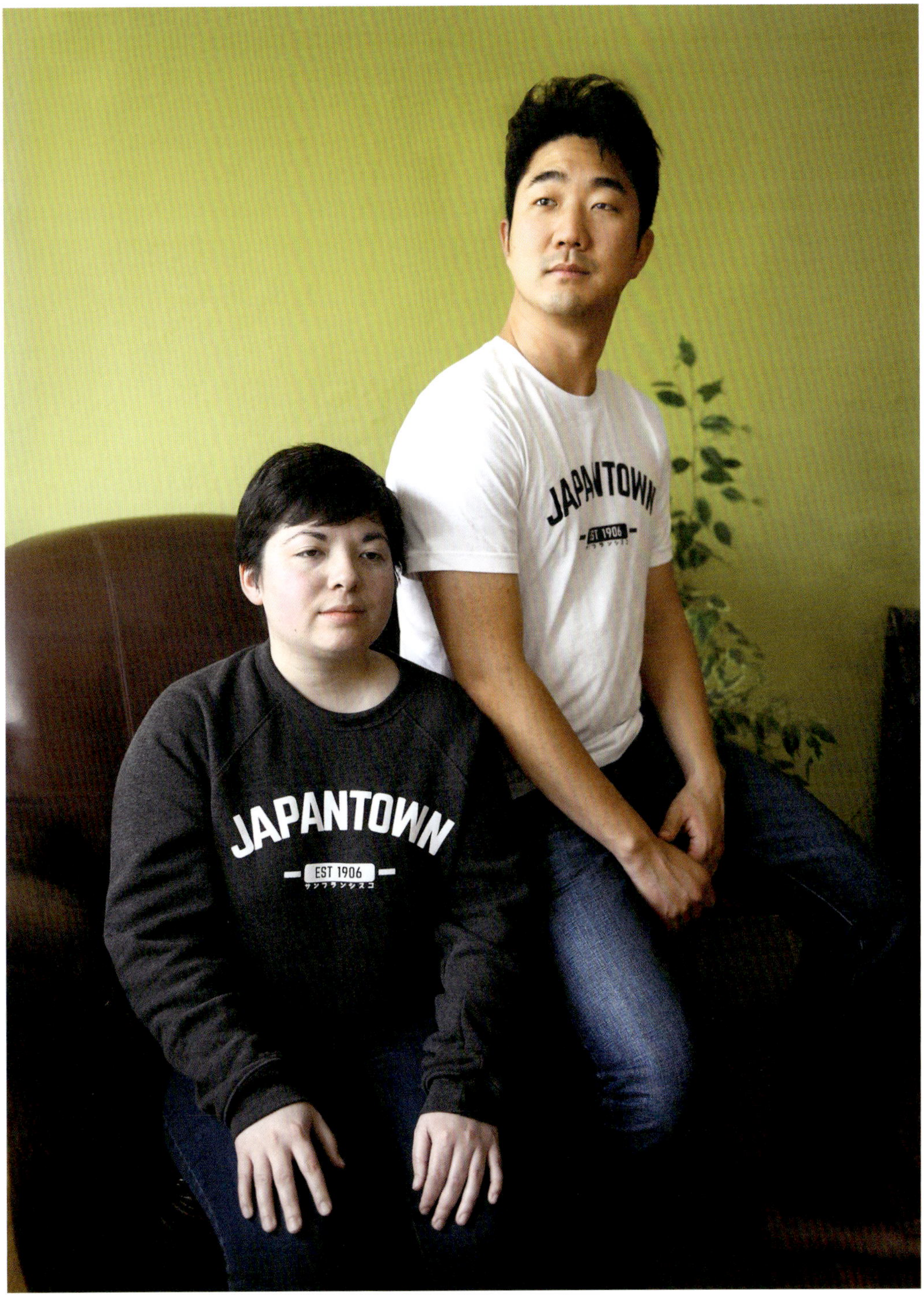
JAPANTOWN
EST 1906
JAPANTOWN
EST 1906

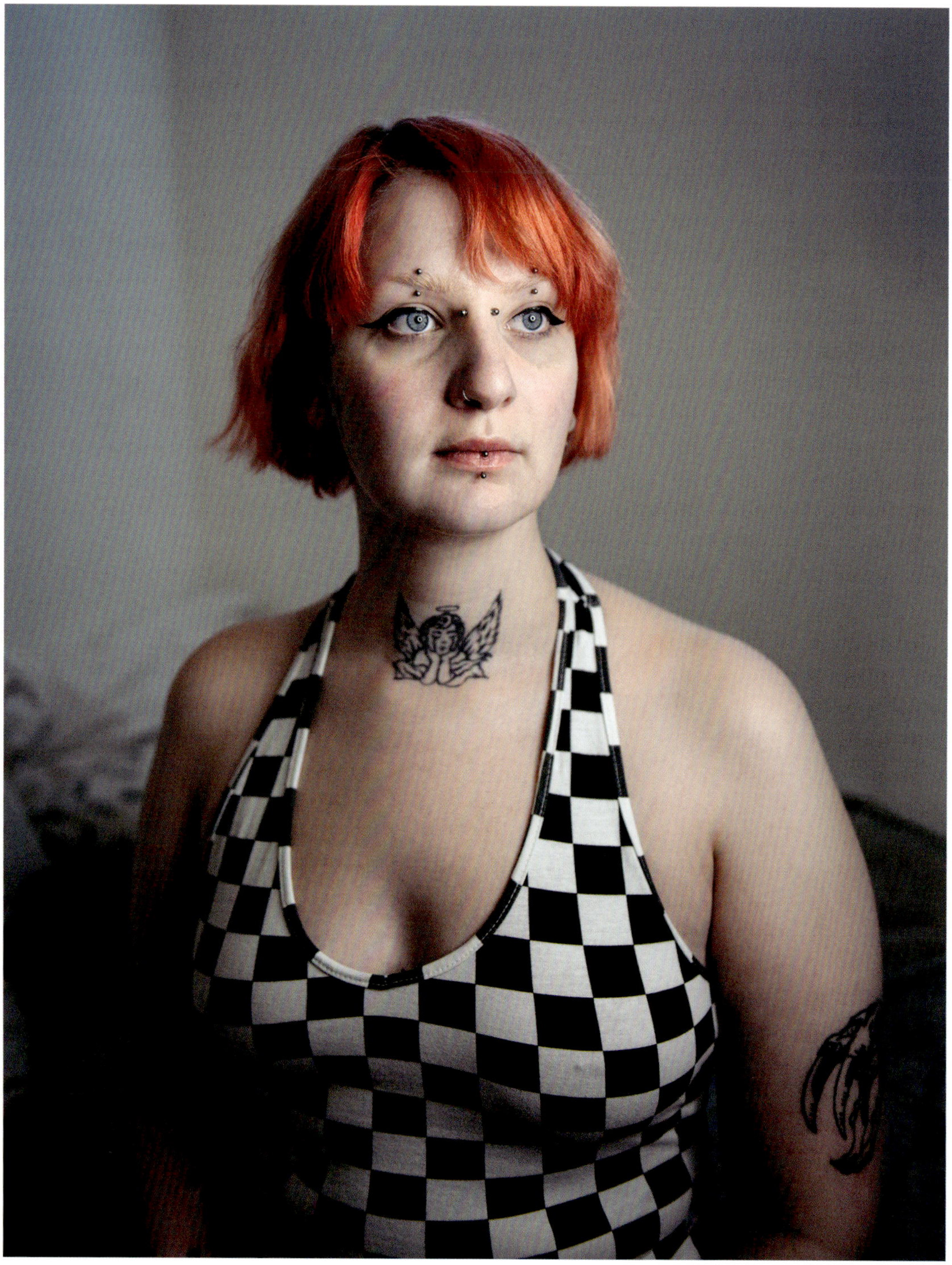

Arna | Reykjavík, Iceland | 2023

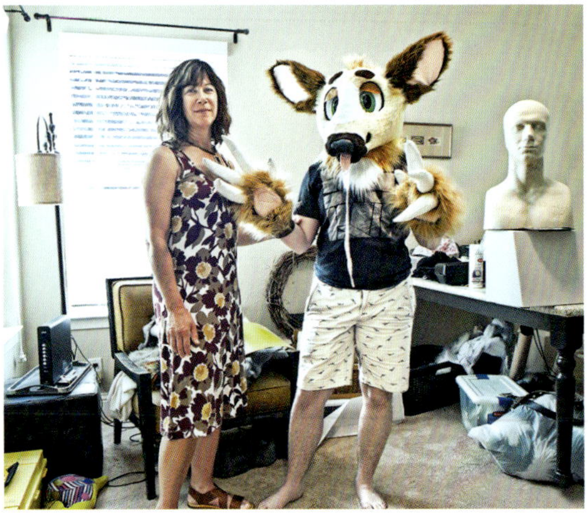

Judy and Leo | Davis, CA | 2016

"When Leo told us that he is transgender I was speechless. Fortunately, my husband knew exactly the right words: we love you. For a time, I was devastated. It felt like my child had died. With time I came to realize that what had died was my own fantasy of what my life with my child would be, but the *person* that I knew and loved was still there. Love is love. Your child is your child is your child.

Leo realized he was transgender after he attended a panel discussion hosted by people in the LGBTQ community. He came out to us, his parents, in middle school, and he told his younger sister a year before. We understand why he wanted to ease the family into this news; coming out didn't only allow him to start transitioning into his true gender, but it also brought the family into our own type of transition.

Leo has always been an outlier. He wasn't into the things most of the other kids in our community were pursuing. I had always assumed that the source of his angst was from having such different interests, but I now know that it is because he was not comfortable in his own skin—literally. He told us that when he went to the discussion, he had an aha moment, and could finally put a name to what he was feeling. He told his sister that his plan was to tell us, and if we weren't accepting, he was going to run away and live with a teacher. His sister planned to ride her bike over after school to visit. When he finally sat us down to talk, I thought, 'OK, she is finally going to tell us that she is a lesbian.' I was prepared for that, but not that he was transgender. His father and I weren't angry. I was in shock. His dad and I spent a lot of time privately crying, and joined a very expensive wine club.

Over time, we learned more about what being trans means. Leo patiently guided us through his experiences and his journey into his true identity. We watched him bloom in ways we couldn't imagine. Sadly, the positive changes forming in his life didn't come without hardship. It was heartbreaking to see how being misgendered and misnamed hurt him.

When he went away for college, he had the chance to start with a clean slate, with no dead identity attached to him. He could be who he was, not what people wanted to see, and that's where his true friendships were made. He has chosen to let go of old relationships because being with some of the people he knew from high school before transitioning reminded him how miserable he felt at that time.

Leo has made us much better people by motivating us to look inward and examine our own biases and ignorance, and for this we will be forever grateful. When Leo came out as trans, he showed us the amazing person he had always been. I compare it to M&Ms: he is a different candy color on the outside but still the same inside. We didn't lose anything; we gained a whole person. And we have since quit that wine club and joined a more modest one."—Judy

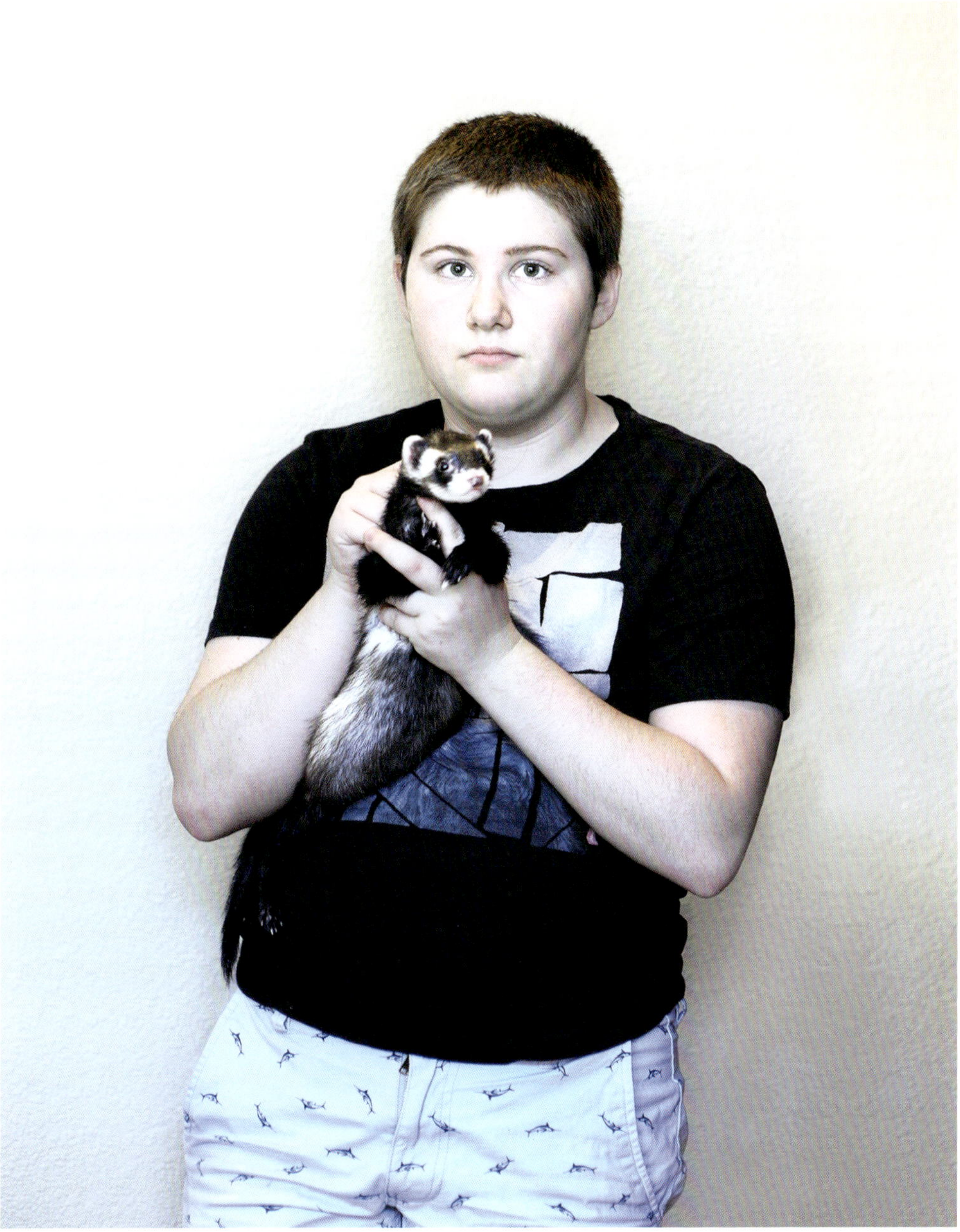

Jeni | San Francisco, CA | 2017

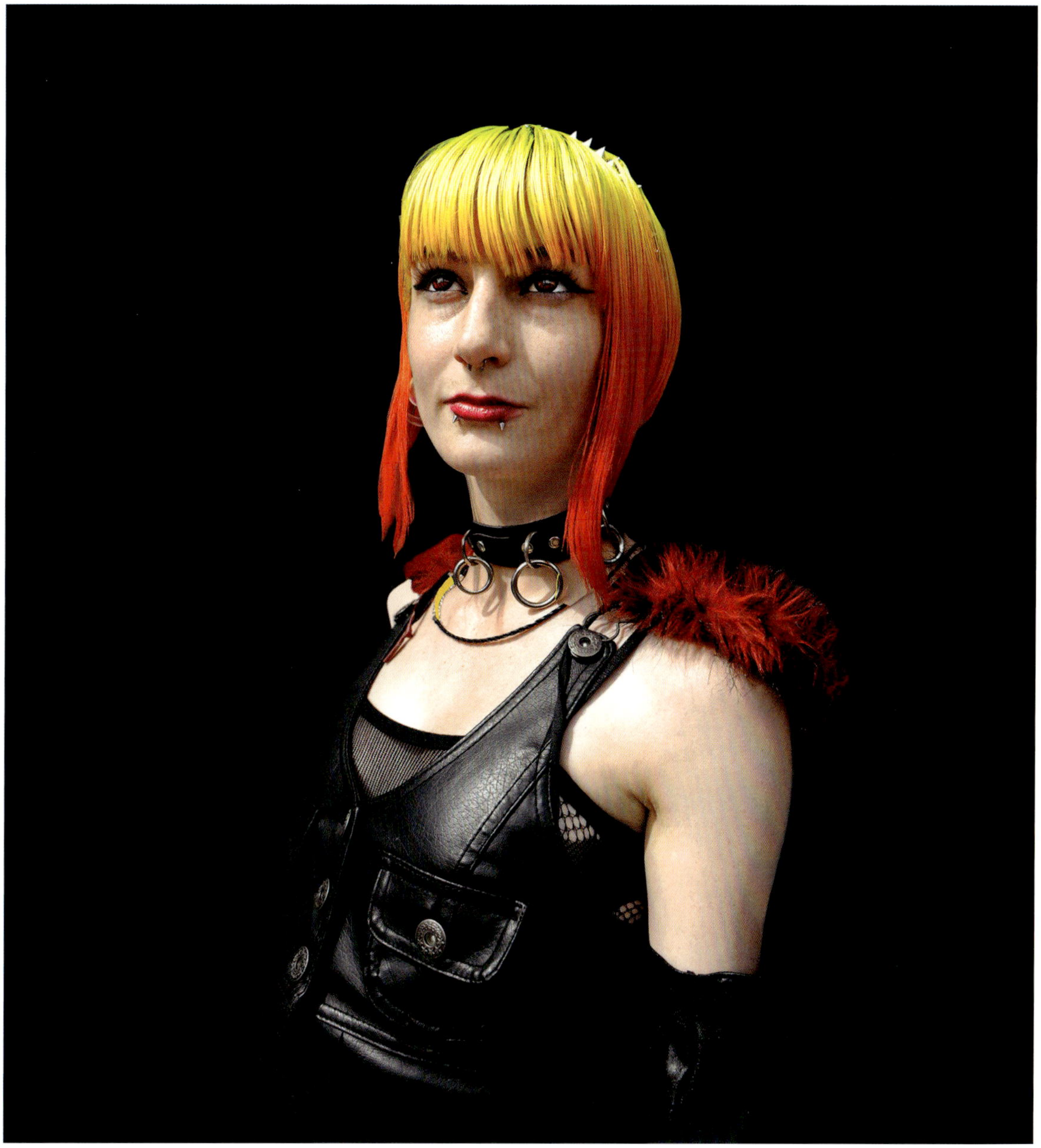

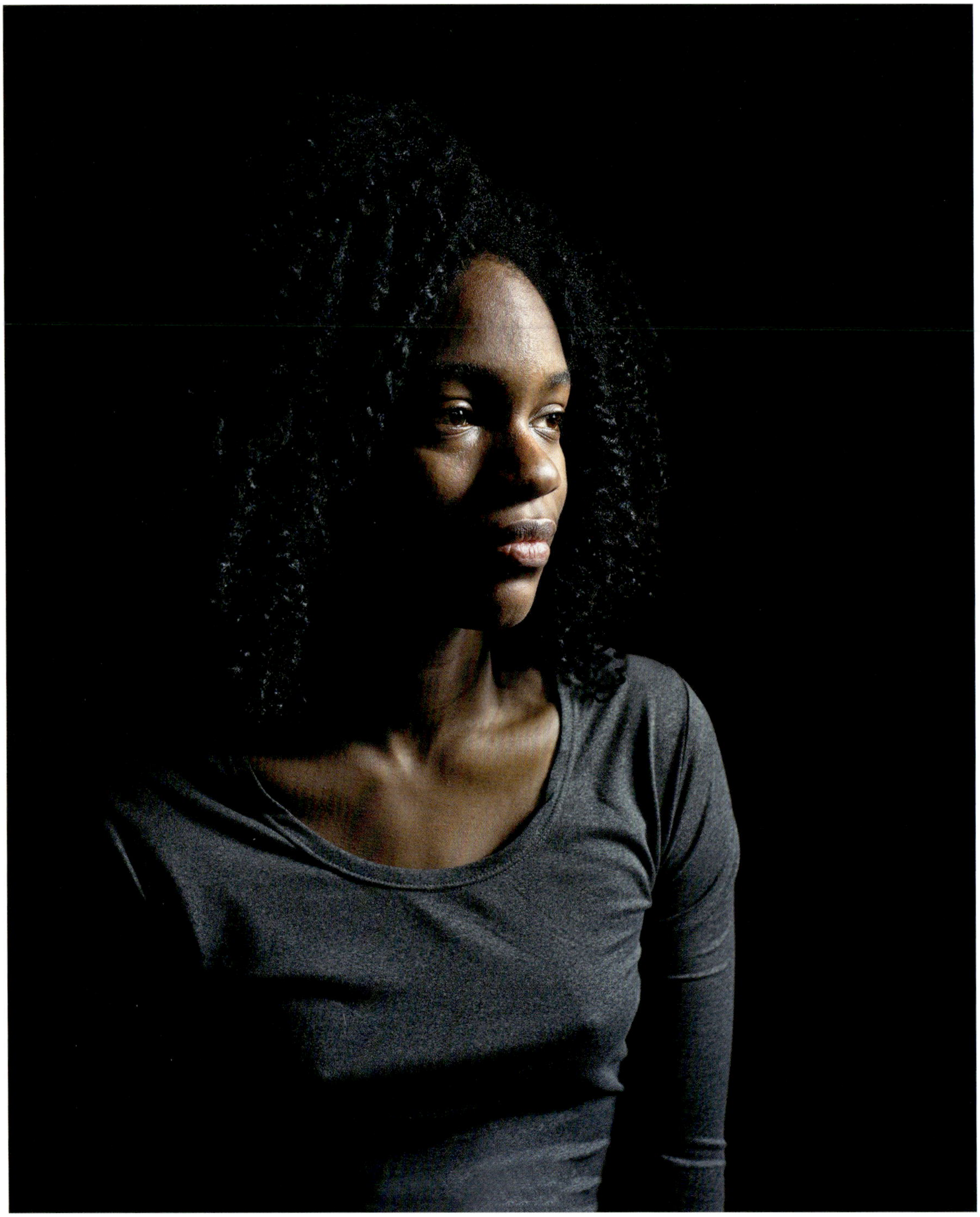

Ari | San Francisco, CA | 2017

Ethan and Cari | Orange County, CA | 2018

"I applaud my son Ethan for being brave—to be who he is and who he is supposed to be. Ethan has accomplished so much in his life, most of which before the age of eighteen. He asked me to take him to his first 'Gay Days' at a local amusement park at the age of thirteen, started a Gay Straight Alliance on his high school campus, and played the lead of his high school musical as his identified gender. He also went to the California state capitol to lobby for the passing of AB 1266, for transgender bathrooms, volunteered for Planned Parenthood, attended the GLAAD Awards, and marched in numerous Pride Parades, specifically the LA Pride Parade with the Rainbow Youth Alliance. It is Ethan's dedication to the education of youth through the lens of human rights coupled with his activism for transgender rights that bring a smile to his face. As a mother, I love Ethan's natural tendency to be compassionate and to volunteer as they are a testament to his caring personality.

Despite his involvement—most of which required me transporting him to and from these events—he struggled to feel supported at home. When Ethan was younger, I came home from work to find him in the bathroom with gashes all over his body, sitting in a pool of blood. It was and continues to be the scariest sight in my world. I wish no parent ever has to experience that. Up until that moment I never heard the word transgender. After having Ethan transported to the hospital, I learned what transgender meant during support group therapy meetings. I also learned my child was still my child, my blood, and the best creation—next to his sister—in my life. My child was still the same person.

The transitioning of pronouns was the most difficult. I was re-learning how to address people with out using he/she, her/his. Whenever I slipped up, Ethan wouldn't speak to me, and he suddenly refused any kind of affection, like hugs or kisses. He couldn't get the legal gender change or surgery without my consent, and he still didn't believe I was supportive of him. We had done so much together, and I was so involved in his life, and now he pulled away and tried to shut me out of his world. A world I support much more than he knew.

Little did he know I was sharing a similar journey but was never strong enough to 'come out.' I was not brave like him. At the age of 48, I took him to a Warped Tour concert and told him I have a girlfriend."
—Cari

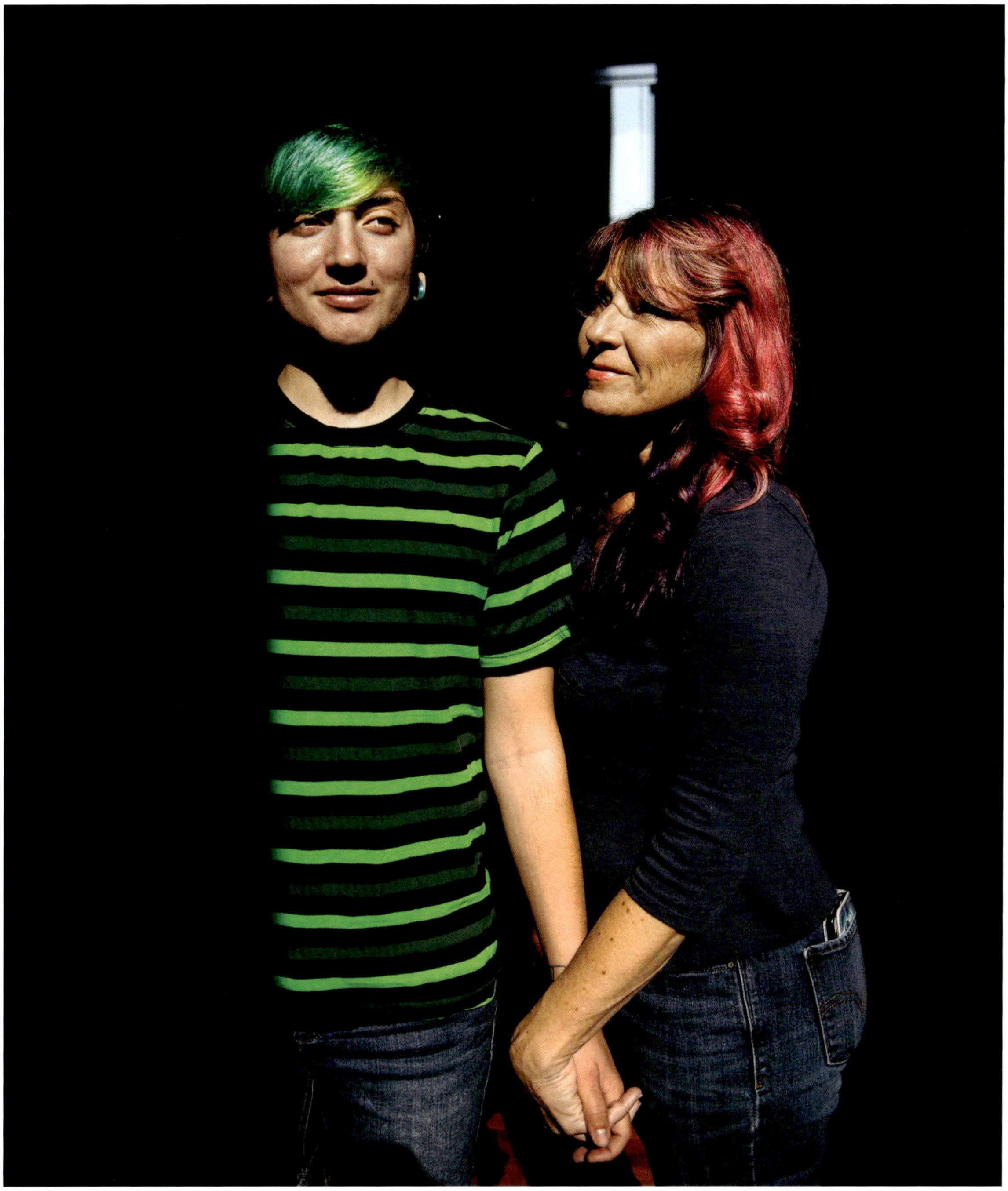

Ethan and Adam (right) | Lafayette, CO | 2023

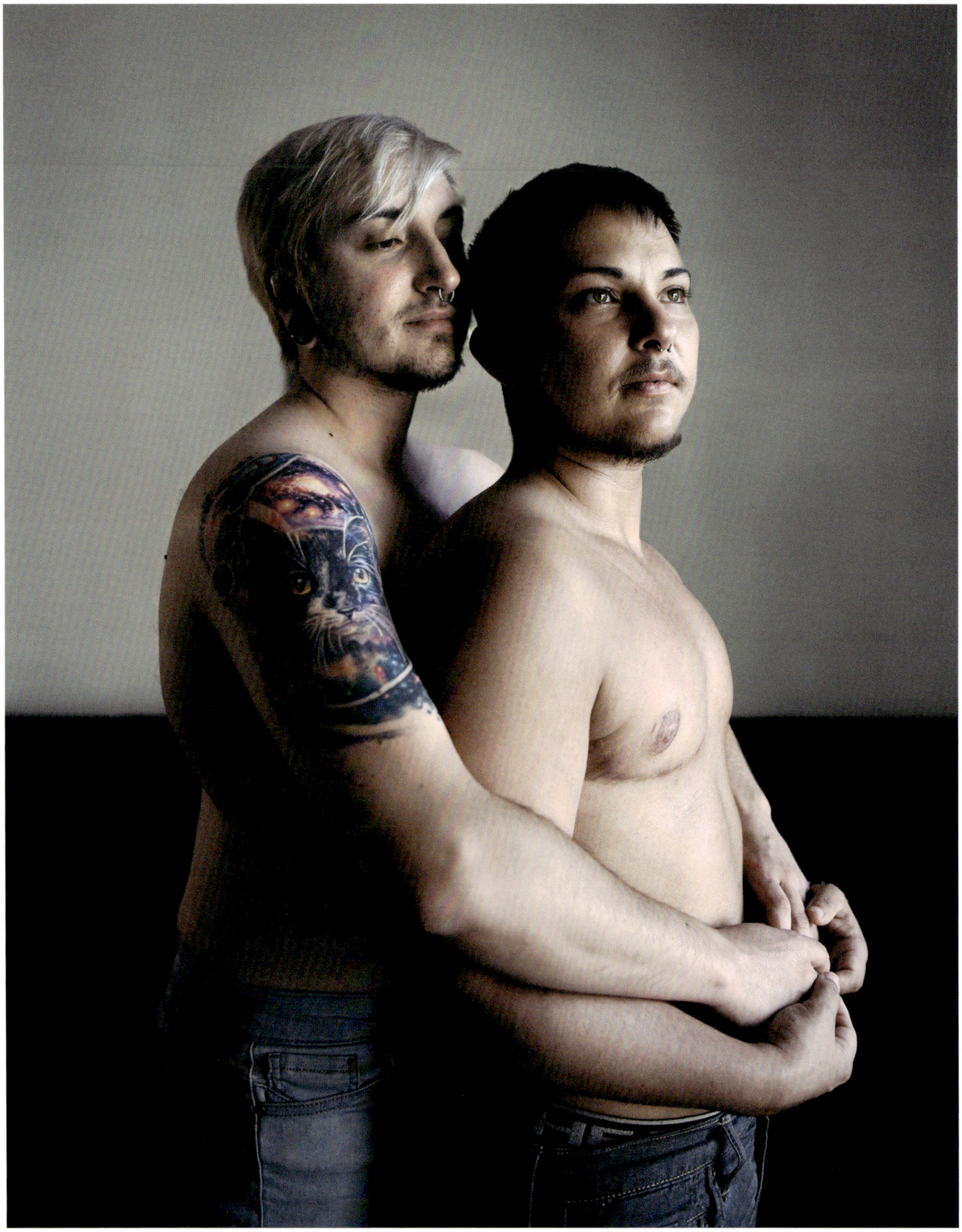

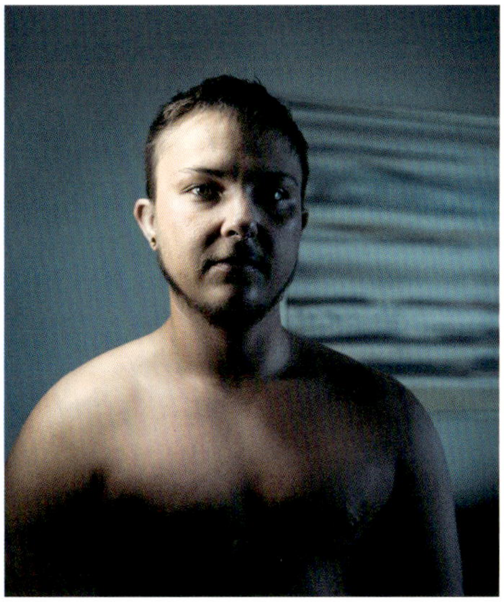

"Taking photos with my husband really captures the essence of queer and trans love. Most of my relationships, even when I was a teenager, have been with other trans folks. I feel most comfortable in these relationships. I admire the strength and courage it takes to live as our authentic visibly trans selves. There's something special about loving someone whose struggle you share."—Ethan

"When it comes to my personal trans experience, it is never a linear 'one size fits all' process. I actually experienced a hyper feminine phase in my life where I was a casino cocktail waitress and even modeled. I was so torn, feeling like I didn't 'deserve' to be trans or I didn't deserve to be a man because of my past. Then I realized, I don't deserve to be trans. I deserve to love myself in my skin and that's all that matters. The past is just that, the past. It's behind me and I will always honor that small blip in my journey, but I will never let it define me every time I look in the mirror. Who cares if it's a 180-degree 'shock' to people around you? I've been spinning in circles all my life trying to fit in. Frankly, this messed up world needs a shock. Don't be afraid to share your spark. Humanity needs it."—Adam

Pat | San Francisco, CA | 2019

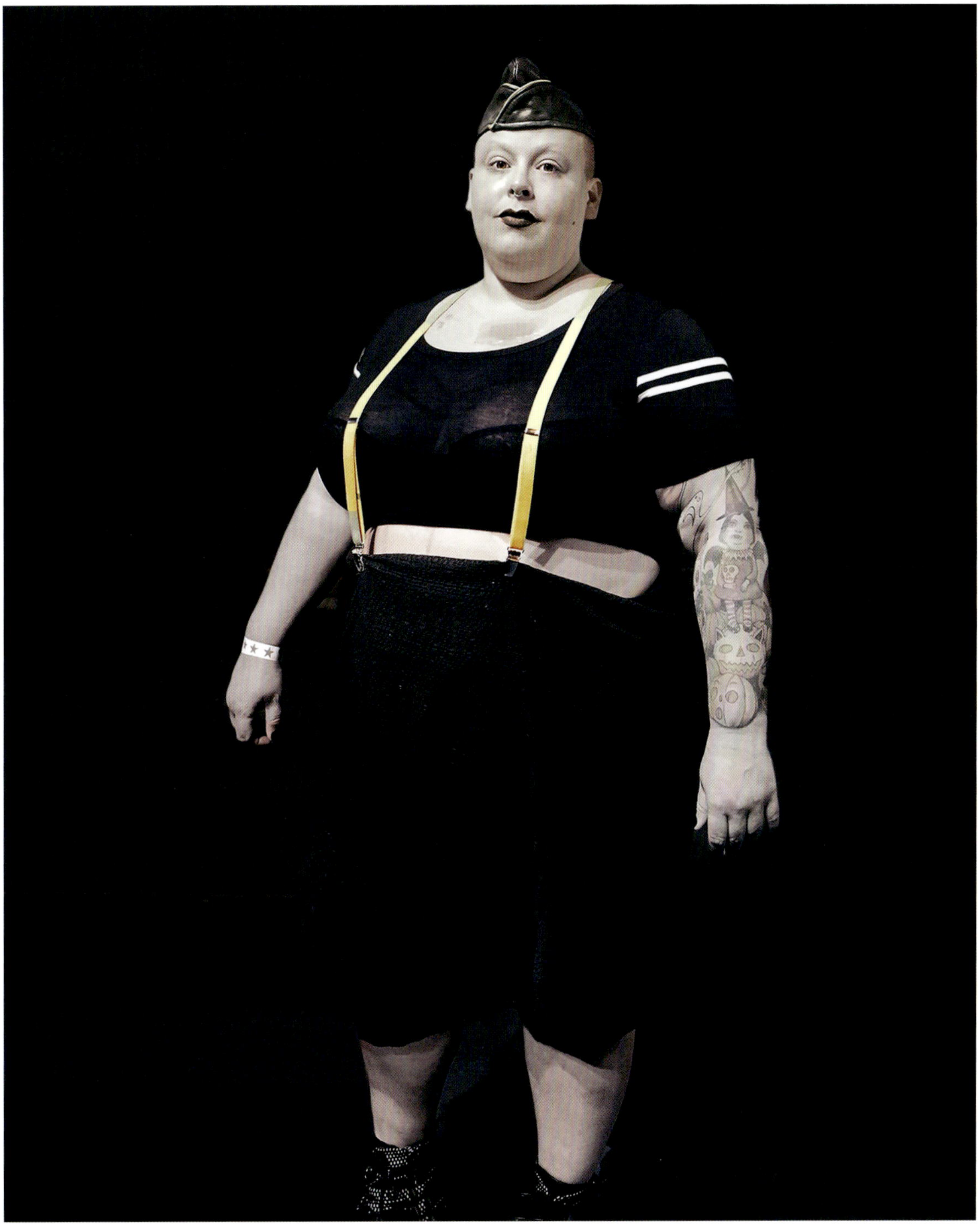

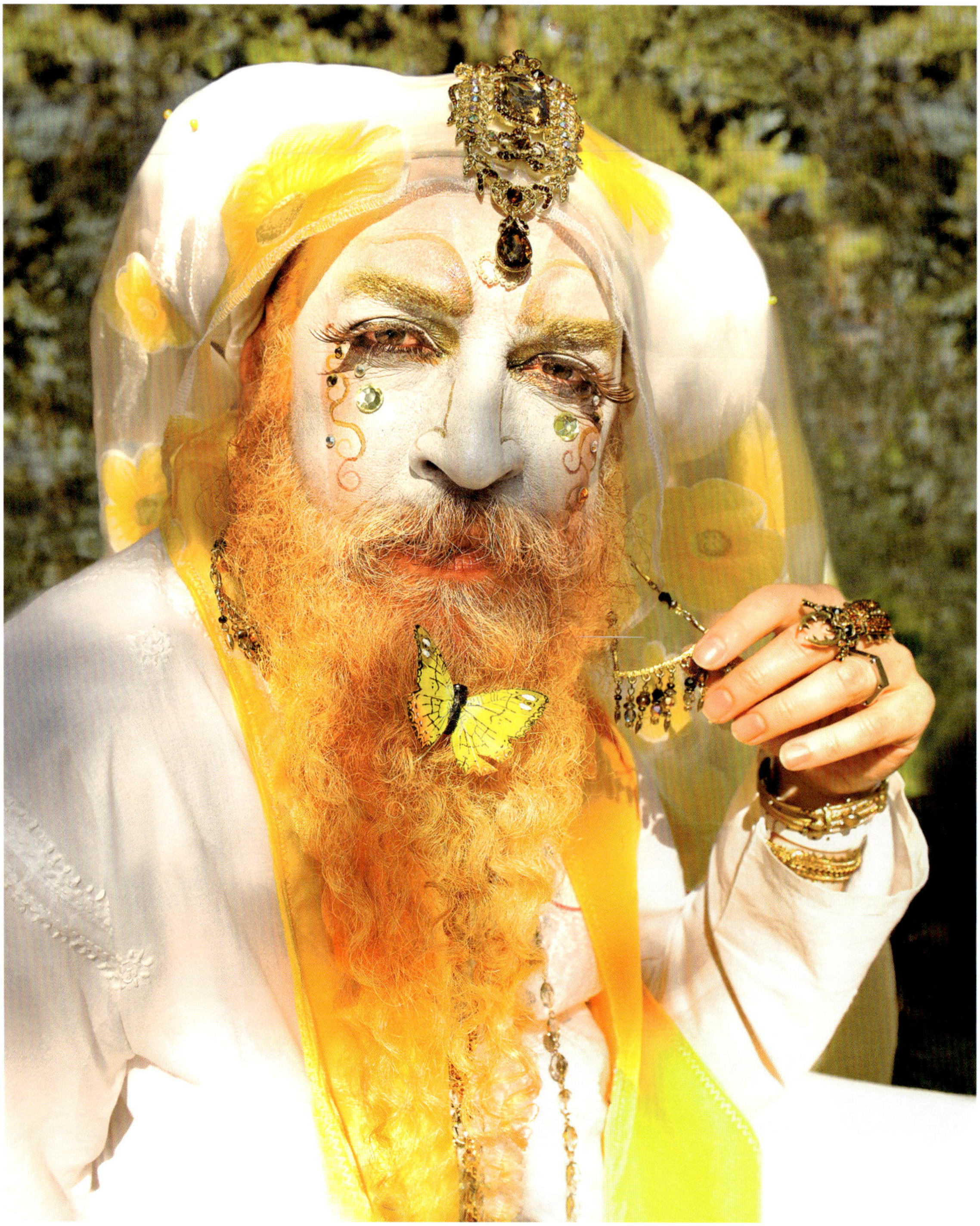

Sister Daisy | San Francisco, CA | 2017

Kathy, Alex, and Lee | Palo Alto, CA | 2018

"When Lee and I met in 1989, people in the LGBTQ community were still closeted, even in areas like Boston, NYC, and San Francisco. We were intentional about coming out to our managers at work and explaining to colleagues our plans to marry and have children. Lee is the birth parent of our two daughters, who are genetic siblings."
—Kathy

"Kathy and I married in 2008 when it became legal in California, even though we'd already had a commitment ceremony in 1992 with vows, ring exchange, and over a hundred guests. Our daughters participated with us in celebrating our 2008 wedding. They're glad that our family feels like every other Bay Area family that has two working parents, two children, and a dog."—Lee

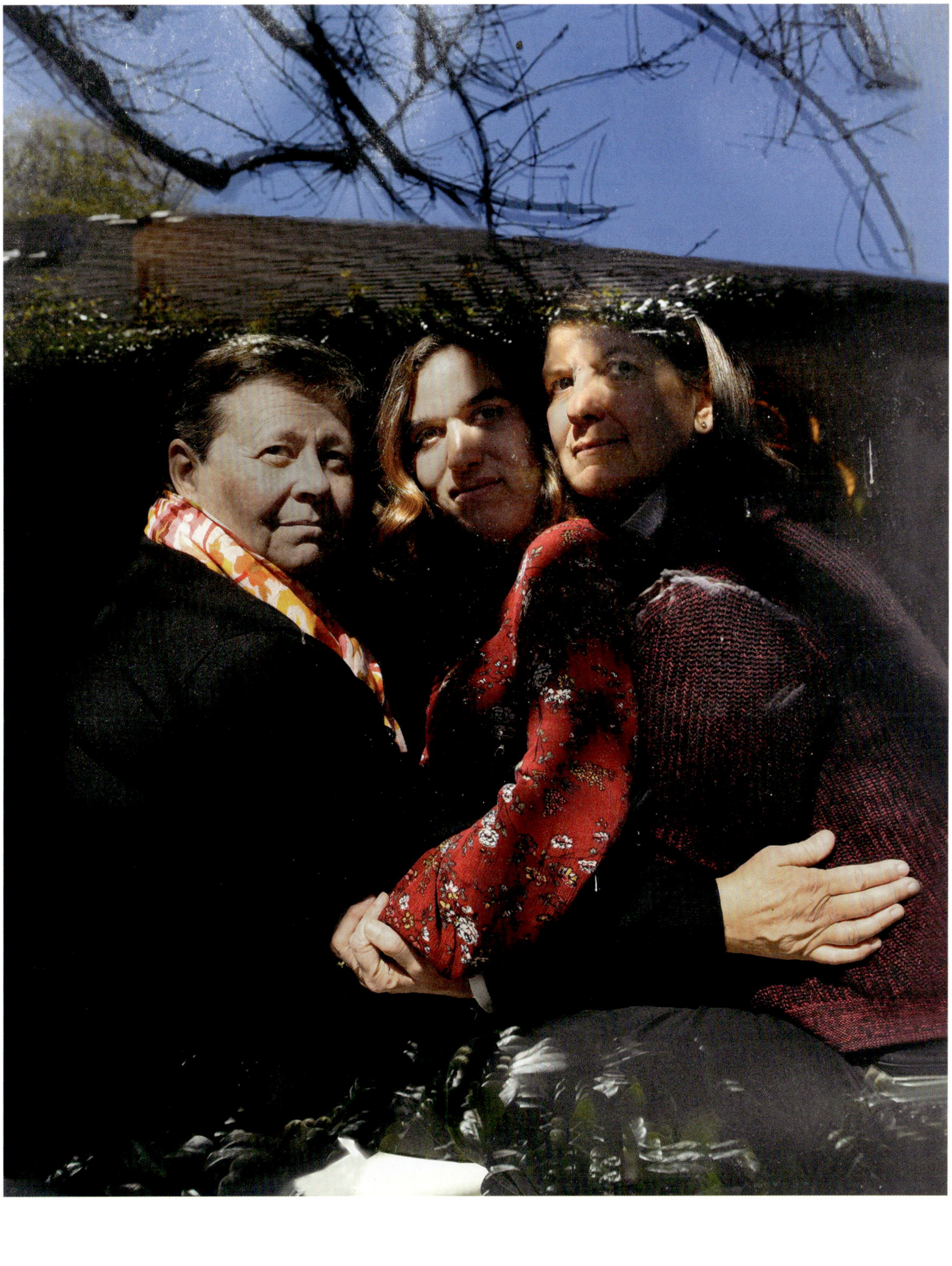

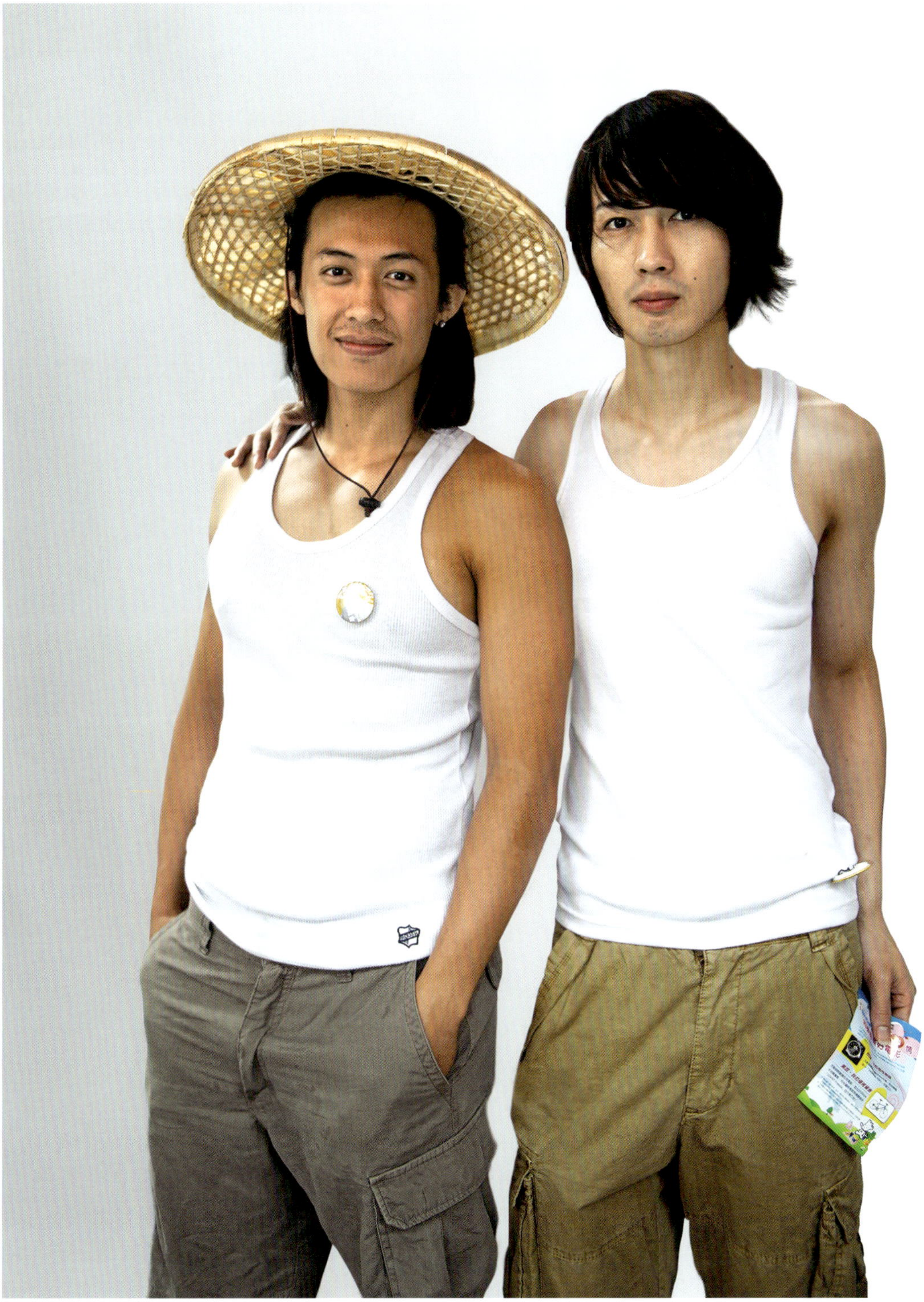

Marianne | San Francisco, CA | 2016

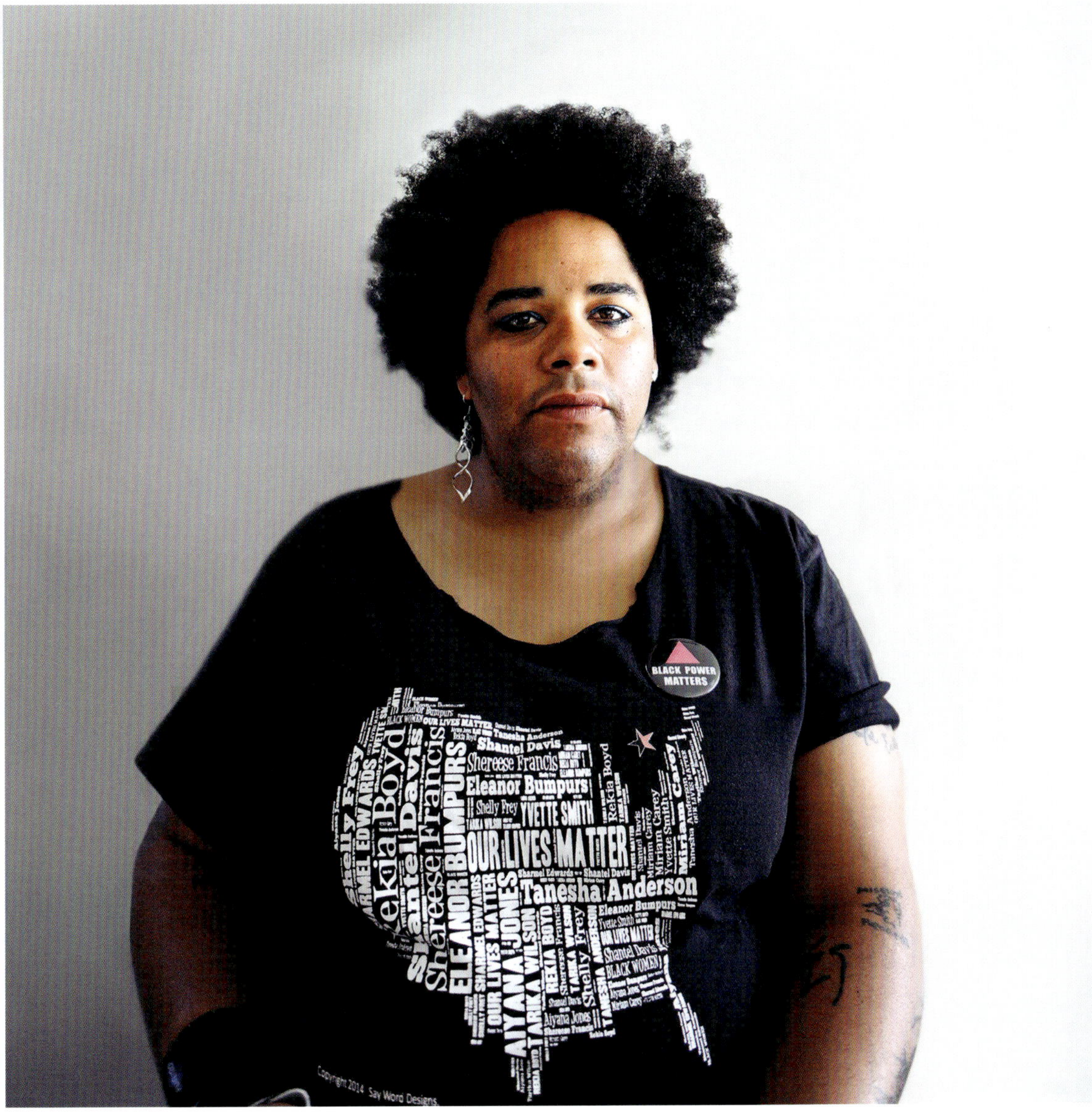
BLACK POWER MATTERS
OUR LIVES MATTER
Tanesha Anderson
Eleanor Bumpurs
Shantel Davis
Shereese Francis
Rekia Boyd
YVETTE SMITH
AIYANA JONES
TARIKA WILSON
Shelly Frey
Copyright 2014 Say Word Designs

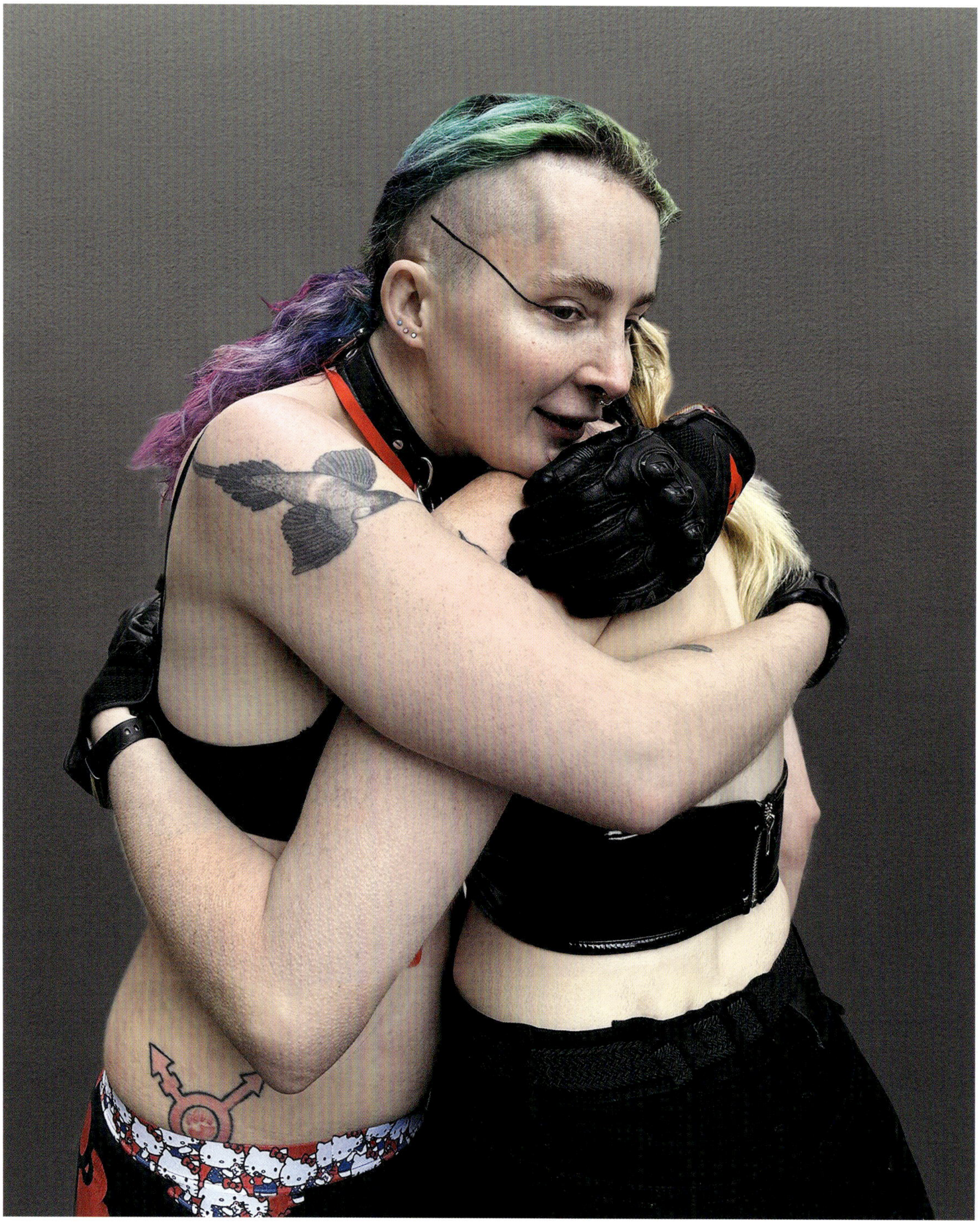

The Embrace | San Francisco, CA | 2023

Sanna and Barkley | Taipei, Taiwan | 2023

"Sanna and I met in the fall of 2003. We were chatting on the Internet and found that we lived very close to each other. We started dating, eating together, and watching movies, just like ordinary heterosexuals. That's how our love started.

Fortunately, we have not encountered any opposition from friends and family around us. Whether at work or in life, we have not encountered discrimination or hatred from anyone. We have been living together for more than ten years. Even though Taiwanese gays could not have the guarantee of marriage, we still lived a low-key, happy life.

In 2016, Sanna went into shock due to excessive blood loss during her menstrual period and was sent to the hospital emergency room. The hospital informed us that an emergency blood transfusion was required and a consent form signed by a direct blood relative was required. I discovered that even after living together for so many years, I couldn't sign her consent form for surgery. I couldn't do anything. I was effectively a stranger—the most familiar stranger to her. Her relatives were not around, so all I could do was to tell her to wake up, to hold her. I felt powerless. I ended up having to signing her name on the consent form on her behalf.

As she was being sent to the operating room, I knew our world needed to change. From 2017 to 2019, we threw ourselves into LGBTQ activism, come rain or shine, telling our story to many people on the streets and letting them know that we need the protection of legal marriage. To me, this was the right thing to do to save lives. Gay marriage was finally legalized in Taiwan in 2019, and we successfully registered our marriage and became a legal gay couple.

In 2022, Sanna suffered another massive blood loss and was sent to the emergency room. This time I had the status of a spouse and could sign the consent form, allowing her to receive medical treatment as soon as possible.

I am very grateful to everyone who worked hard for the LGTBQ movement. Thank you, too, to the Taiwanese government for facing up to the pressures from major religions and becoming the first in Asia to approve gay marriage. The world is still beautiful."—Barkley

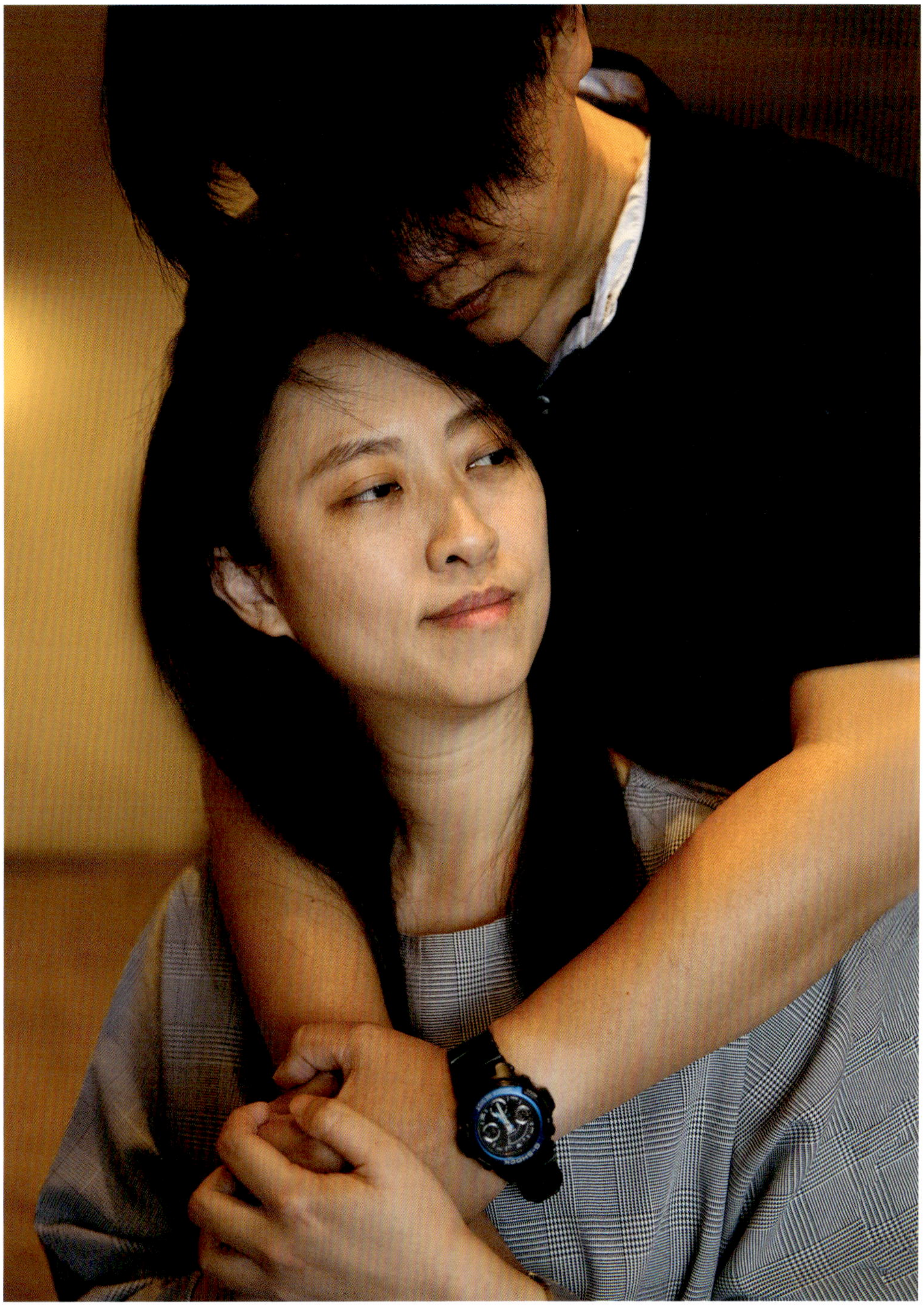

Doug and Jeff
San Francisco, CA | 2023

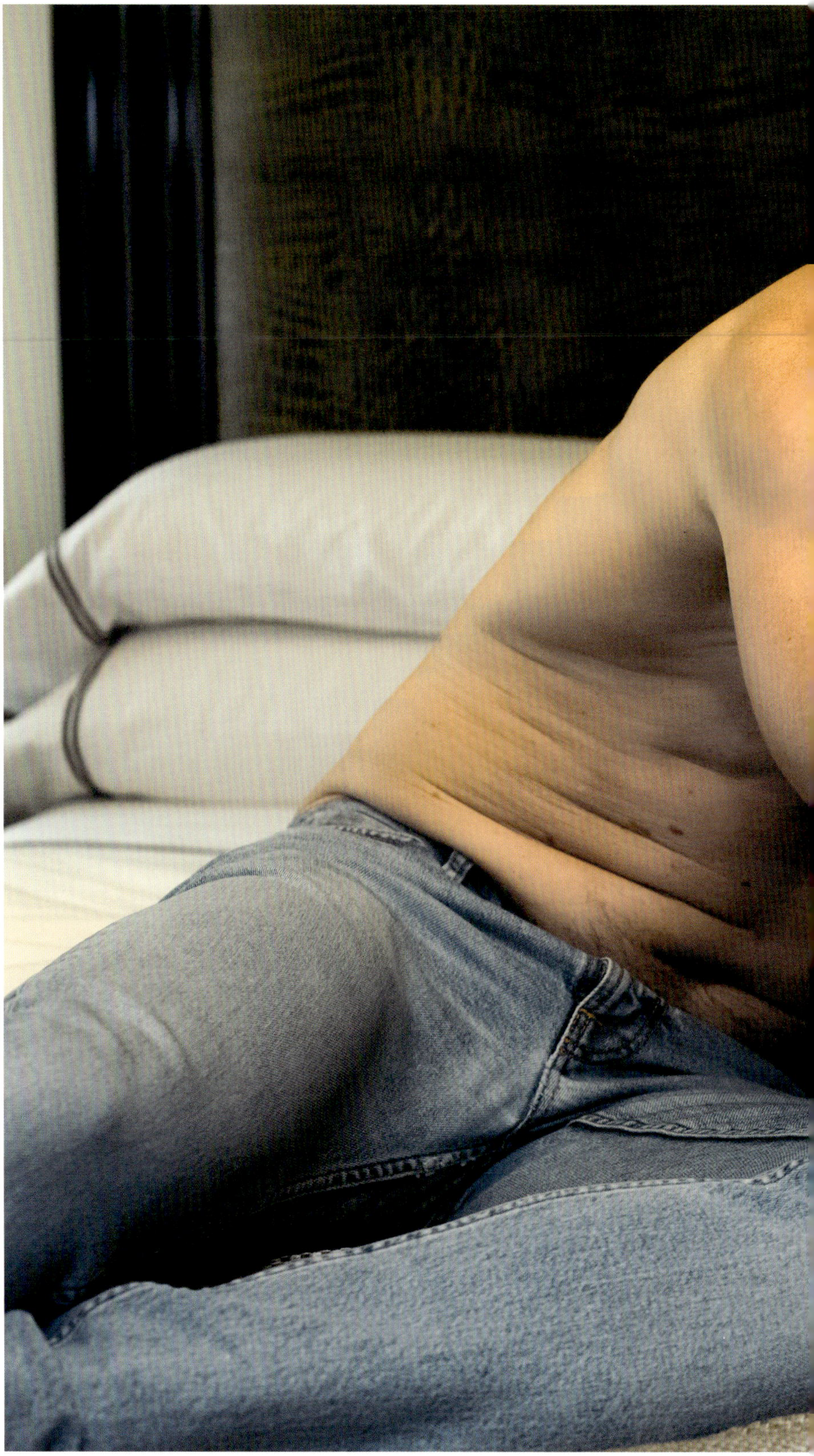

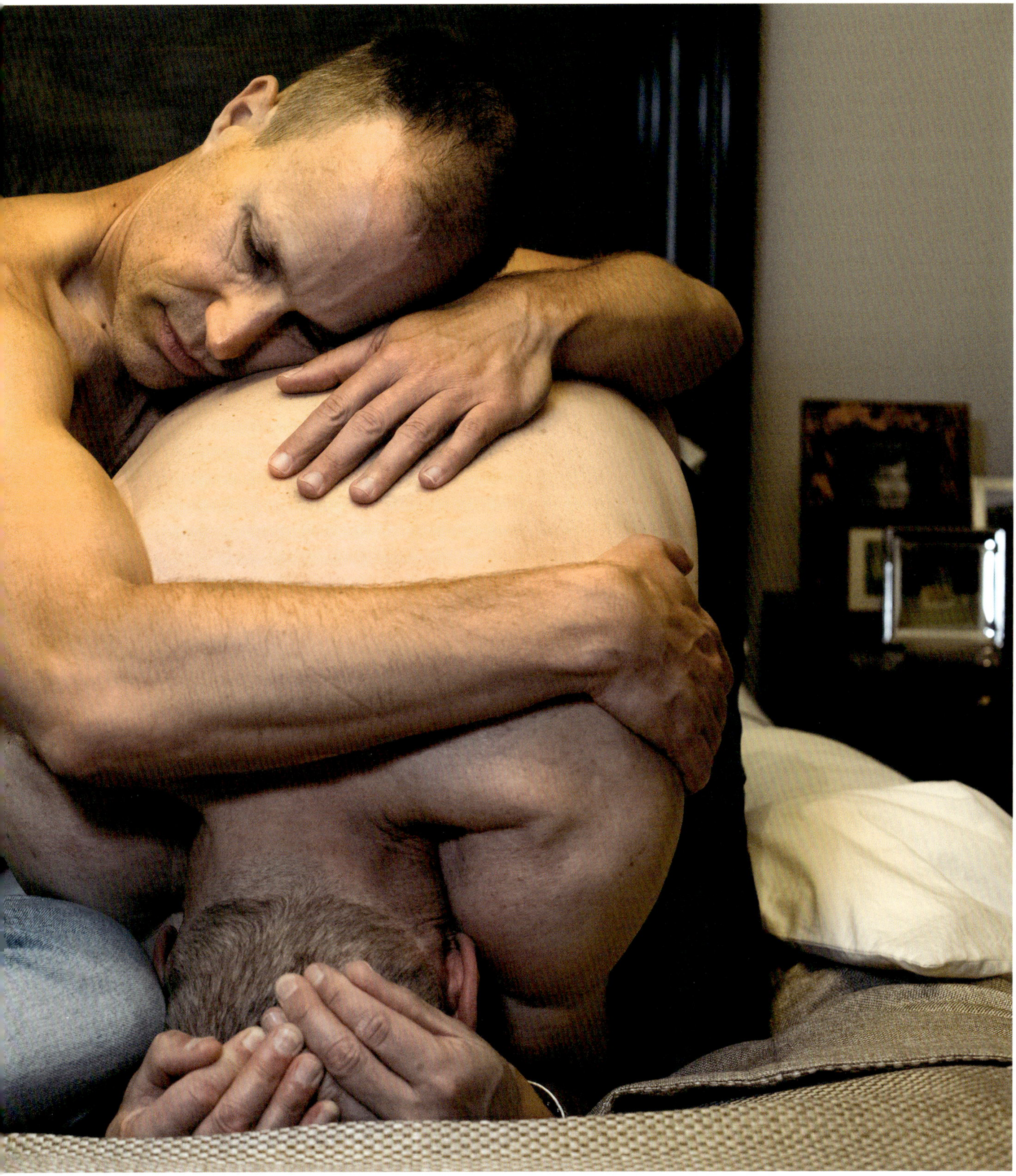

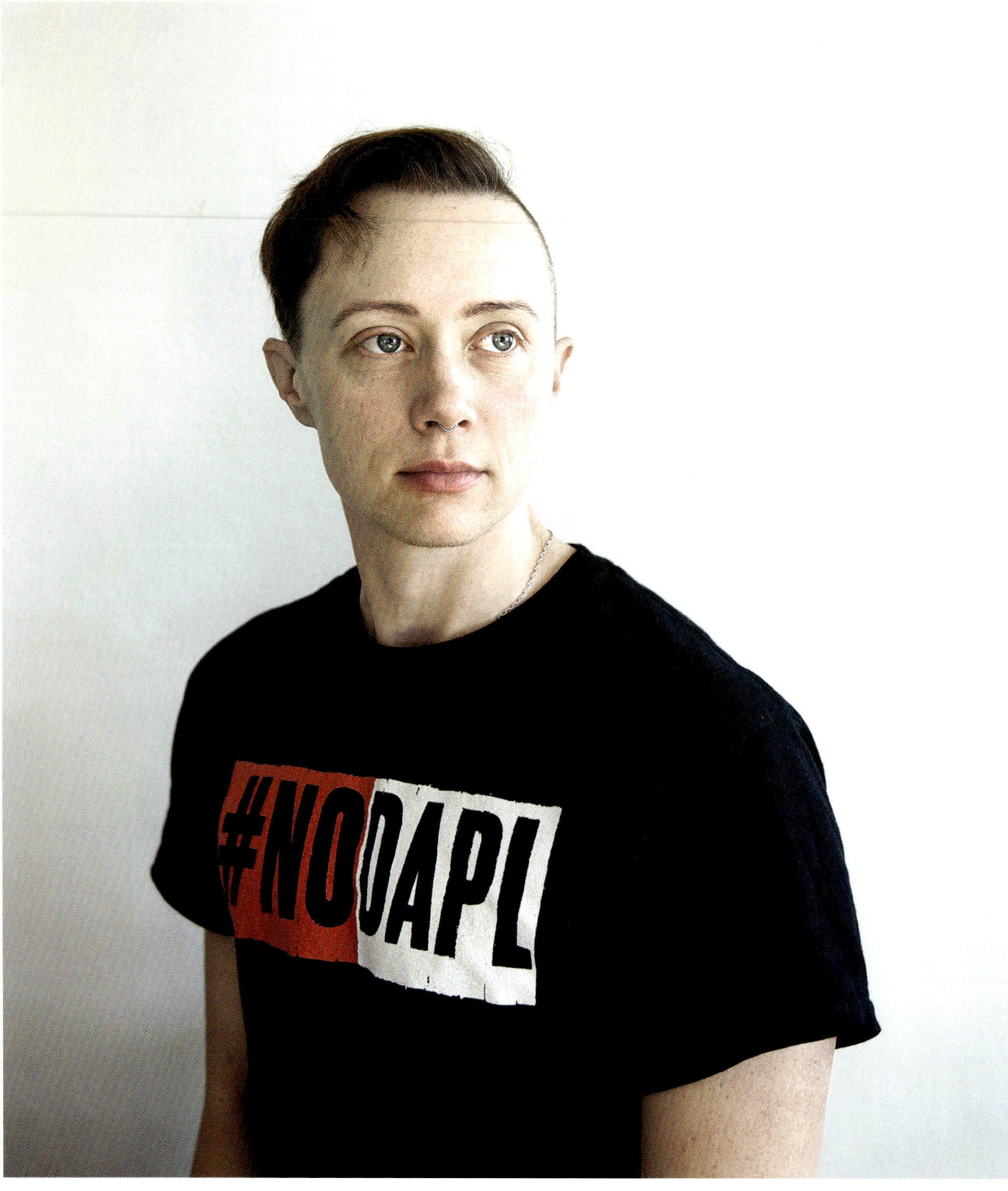
#NODAPL

Emmet | Oakland, CA | 2017

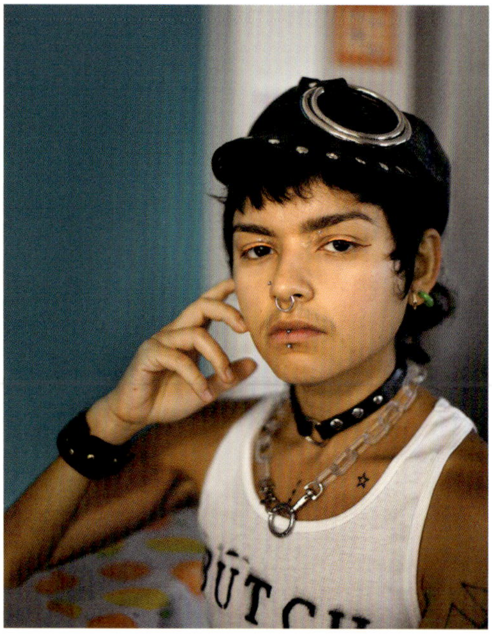

Mono and Elian | Long Beach, CA | 2023

"One of the bigger challenges I've faced as a homosexual and trans individual is security for the future; I am continually worried about my job and emotional security. I often worry about loneliness, and where I can end up if I'm not careful in how I navigate the everyday. As a visibly more androgynous person, in a visibly gay relationship, I navigate my every day with more scrutiny. I would like to some day live in a world where my visibility doesn't put a target on my back or warrant awkwardness from my peers.

I grew up in the Bay Area. I knew that I was gay when I was thirteen. I started to question my gender when I was fourteen. Although I have gone through multiple labels, I feel that my baseline feelings have not changed. I am only finding more and more words to help describe my experience. It took a while, but my mom and dad began to not just tolerate me, but embrace me when I was twenty-three. It took a lot of struggle, hiding my partnerships, and continual arguing.

One day my mother took me aside after I'd asked her why she stopped wanting me to be cis and heterosexual. She told me that she realized that love is already so hard enough to find in this life, and that the people who are lucky enough to have a partnership should be able to enjoy it with no worry. I was so grateful to finally see eye to eye with my mother, who I'd begged to love me for so long."—Mono

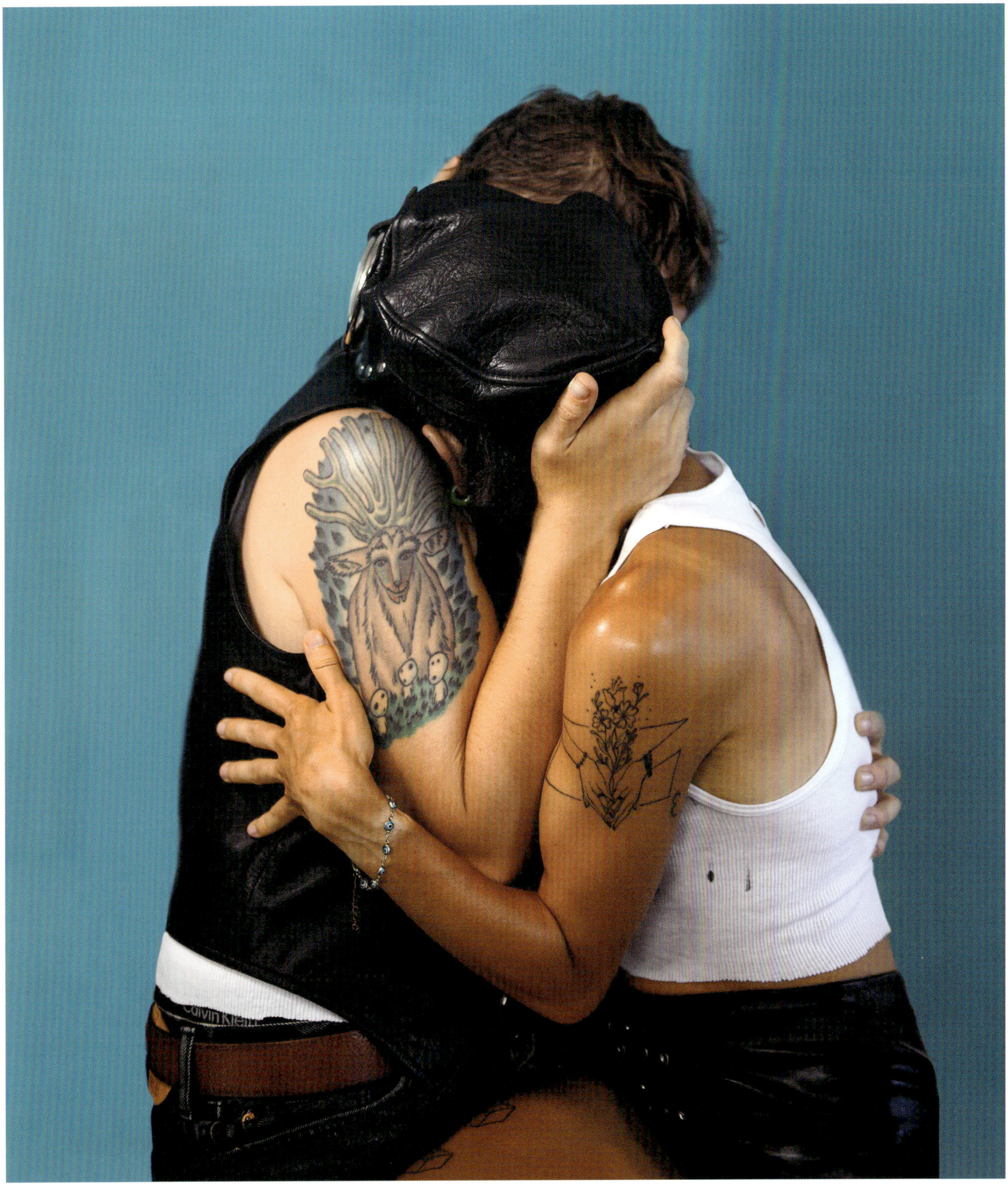

Margrét | Reykjavík, Iceland | 2023

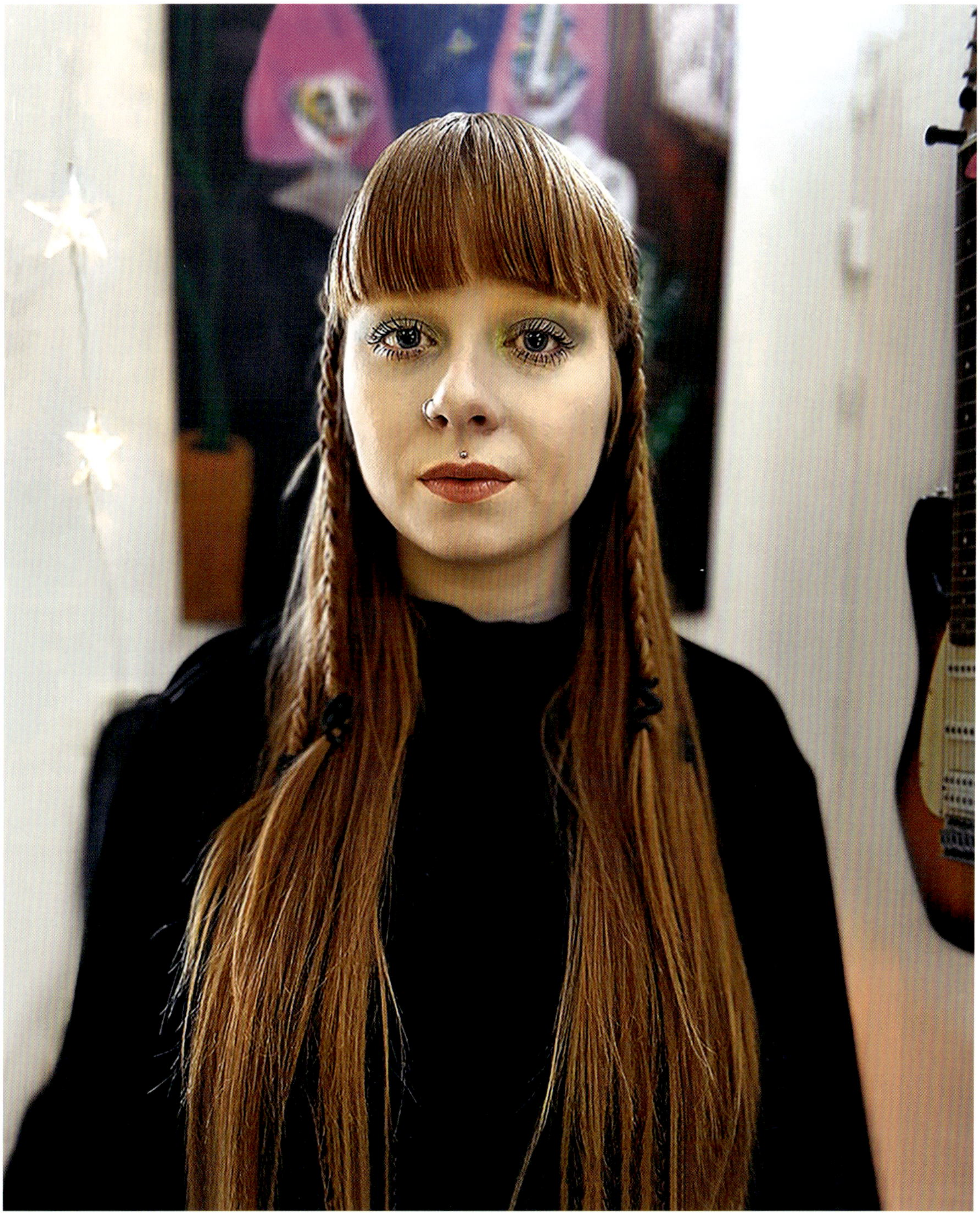

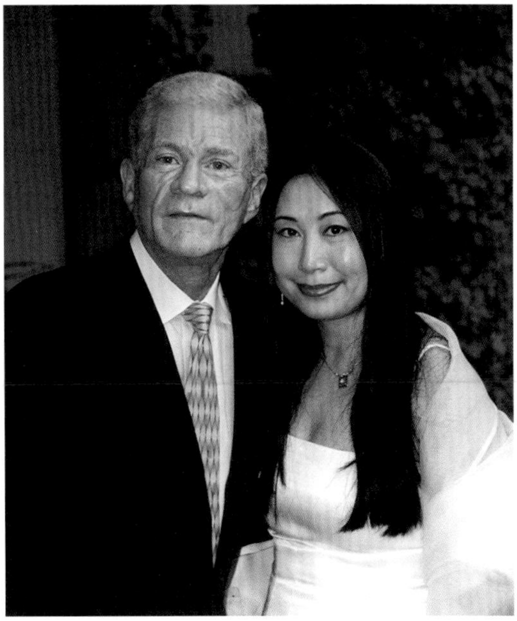

Keith and Sandra | San Francisco, CA | 2017

"On a dark Halloween night, I walked into an old nineteenth-century Victorian house and was met with his tender deep-blue eyes and his face that looked like it had been chiseled from stone. I was happy this would be my new home to share with Keith at this turning point in my life in San Francisco. I was the only straight woman in the house. All our roommates were gay: figure skaters and entrepreneurs in the gay community. We had a lot in common—not only were we both Sagittarians but we also enjoyed beautiful things, such as art, antiques, music, and gardening. I remember singing 'All I Ask for You' from *The Phantom of the Opera* together as Keith played his grand piano. The music helped us both as we tried to recover from our broken hearts and sadness. I became his confidant and true friend. We became life-long friends even after I had moved away. He walked me down the aisle on my wedding day.

Keith lived a very colorful and busy social life surrounded by friends, enjoying his martini after work every day with Frisco, his white cockatiel. One day he told me to my surprise: you are the only friend I have, everyone else has left. I was utterly heartbroken when I learned of his unexpected passing in 2018 just as I was planning to visit him in San Francisco."—Sandra

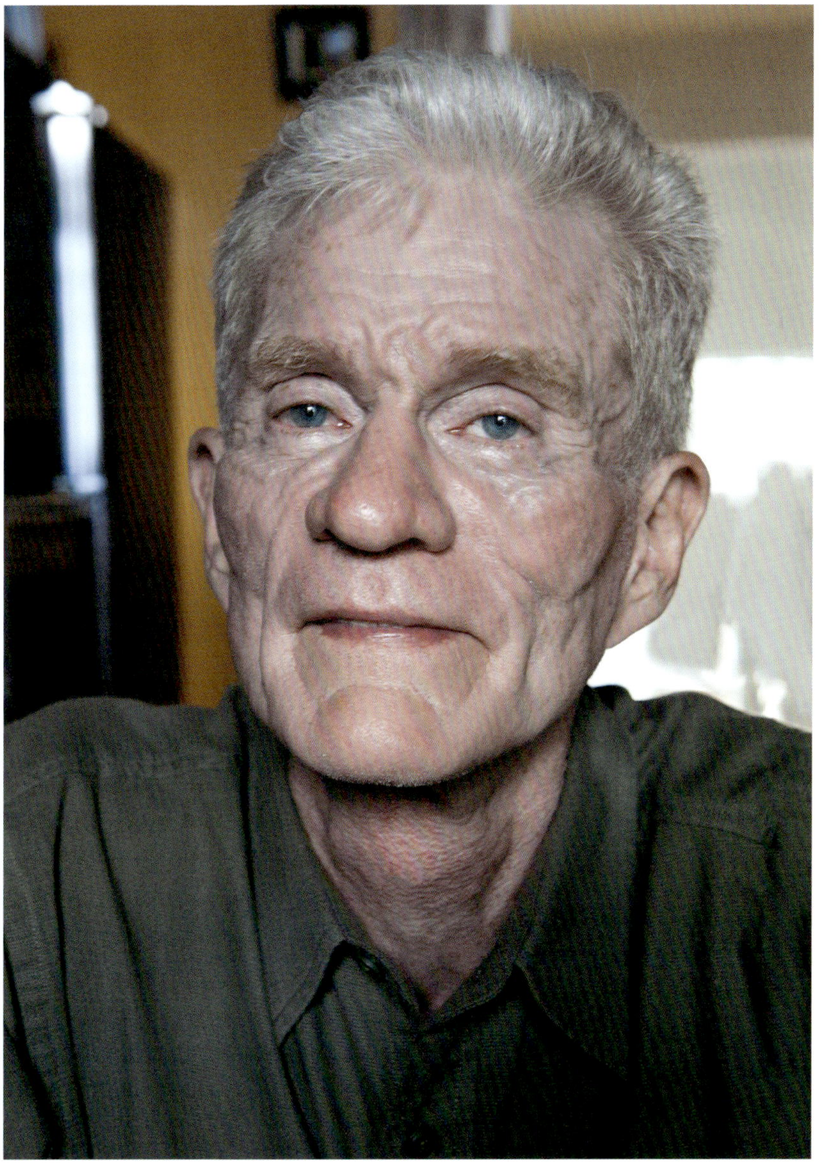

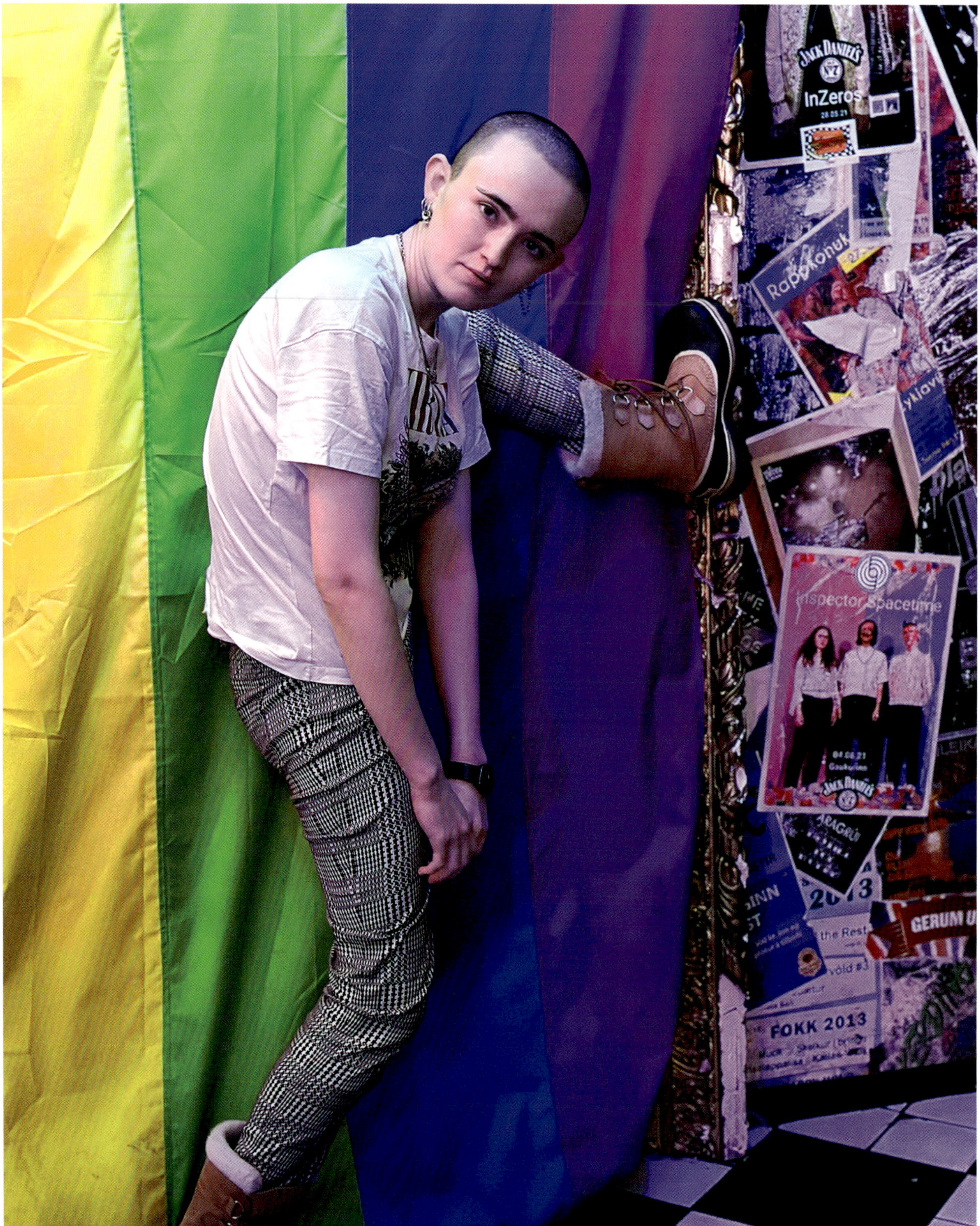
JACK DANIEL'S
InZeros
Inspector Spacetime
JACK DANIEL'S
FOKK 2013

Sadie | Reykjavík, Iceland | 2023

Kyle | Los Angeles, CA | 2023

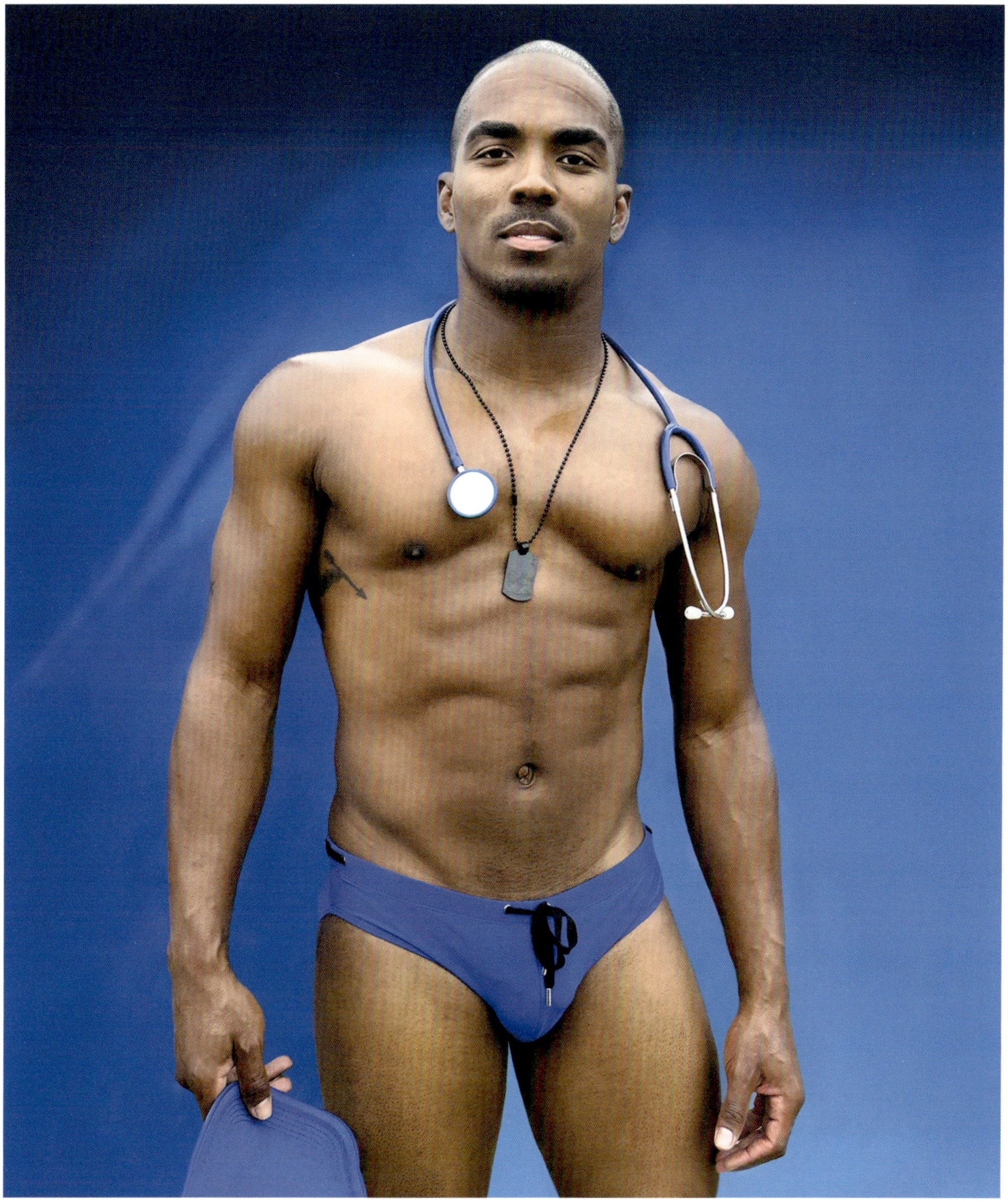

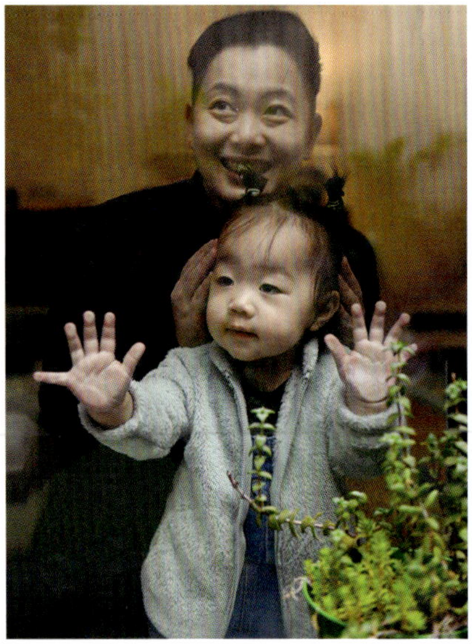

Kim, July, and Morgan | Melbourne, Australia | 2023

Born in the mid-eighties in Malaysia, Kim spent the majority of his formative years growing up in spaces where he felt that he did not belong. Assigned female at birth, Kim knew, from when he was two-and-a-half, that there was an incongruence to the gender he had been assigned. Growing up in a traditional Chinese family in a majority conservative Muslim country, Kim repressed these feelings of wanting to be a boy, conforming to what was expected of him to survive and to meet the expectations of his family.

Moving to Australia in his mid-twenties to study, Kim started to set down roots in Melbourne with the dream of finding his community and sense of belonging. After years of study, working, and dating as a queer woman, Kim reconnected with his high school sweetheart July and proposed the possibility of them being more than friends. Before they agreed to start dating they had a heart-to-heart talk about what was important to them as partners in a relationship, and Kim decided to come out to July that he identified as trans and wanted to affirm his gender in the near future. This was a big step for Kim because July was the first person he had ever come out to as trans. July was surprised—they had known each other for more than thirteen years by this stage—but she was fully supportive of Kim and his journey toward becoming his most authentic self. July eventually left Malaysia and moved to Melbourne to be together with Kim, where they eventually got married in 2019.

Having children was something that was very important to July. After Kim and July got married they started going to the fertility center to try to conceive a child. Unfortunately, despite trying a few times, they were unsuccessful, and July experienced a few miscarriages. Eventually, Kim paused his hormone treatment therapy to see if he could get pregnant, which he did, giving birth to Morgan in March 2022 via C-section after his third IVF procedure. Since then, both July and Kim have been dedicated parents to their bundle of joy.

Being away from family in Southeast Asia during the pandemic was extremely difficult while raising a newborn baby, but with chosen family and a supportive network of friends in Australia, they were able to weather the many storms. Since Morgan was six months old, the new family of three has traveled twice to visit Kim's relatives in Malaysia, as well as to Indonesia to spend time with July's family. Seeing both of their families love Morgan means a lot to them. Time with aging parents and Kim's last living grandparents is precious.

For Kim and July, sharing the story of their journeys carries a powerful message of positive queer Asian representation. Despite the many challenges and barriers they have had to overcome, theirs is an unshakable strength bonded by love.

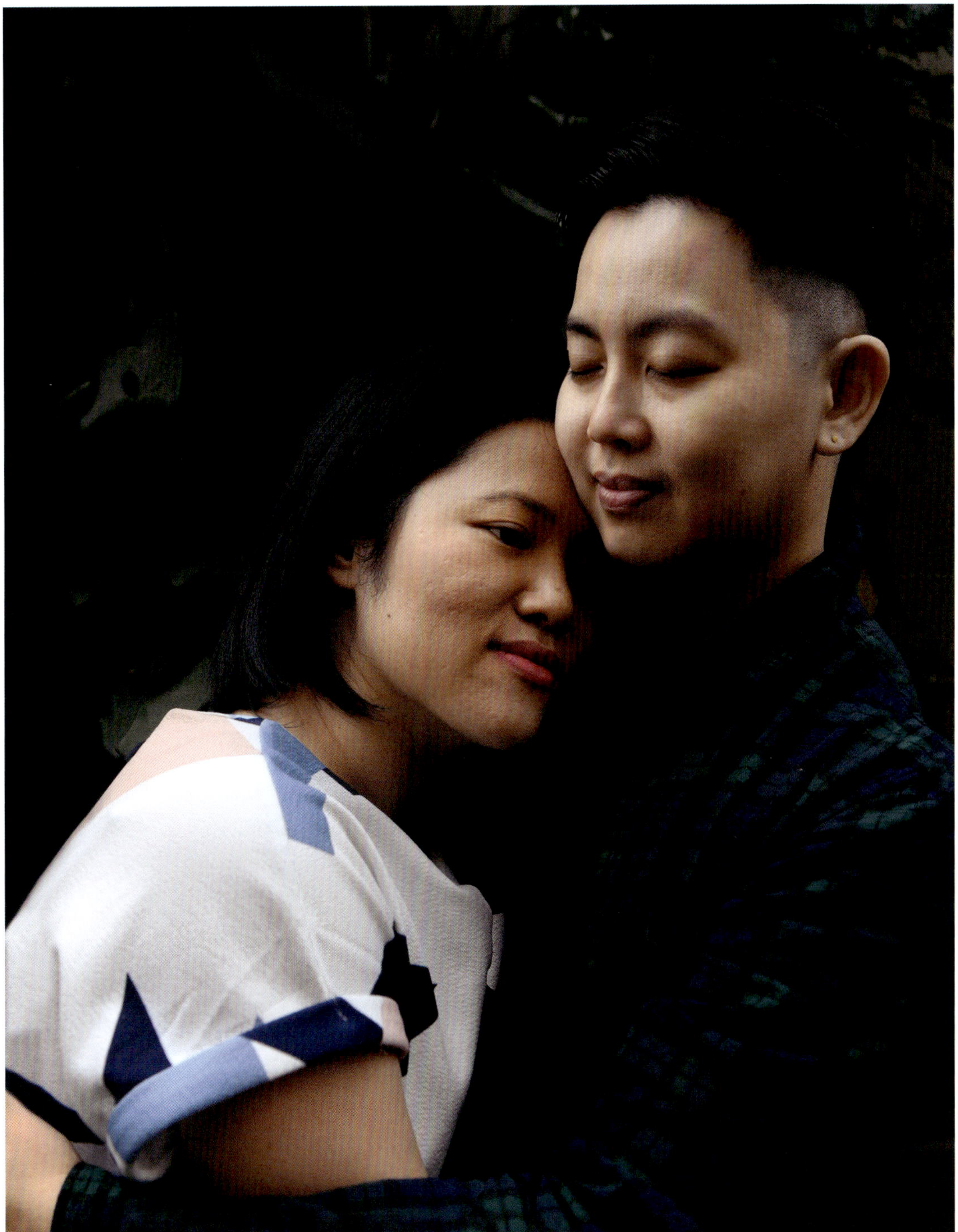

The Bride | Tokyo, Japan | 2019

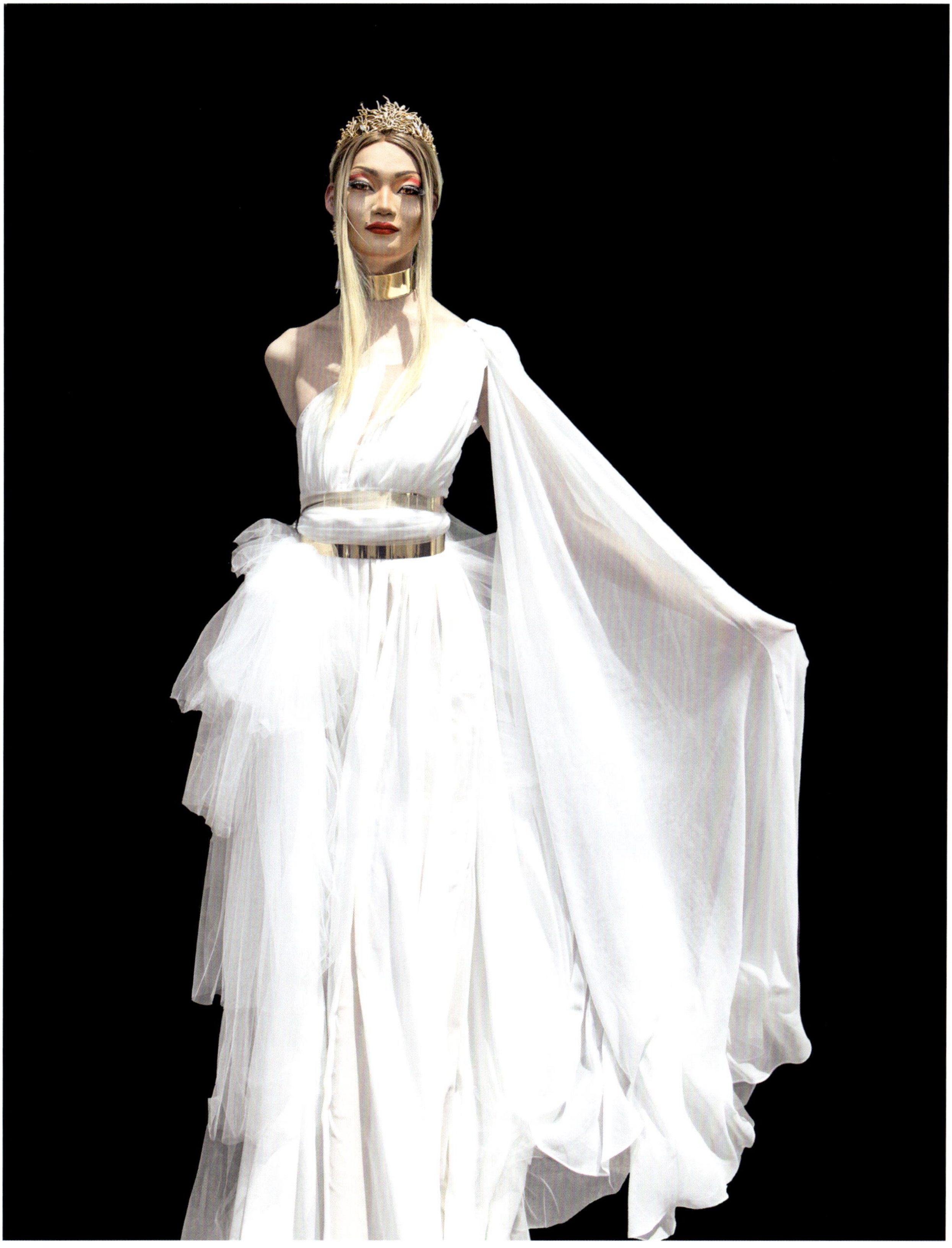

Michael and Kaden | Los Angeles, CA | 2023

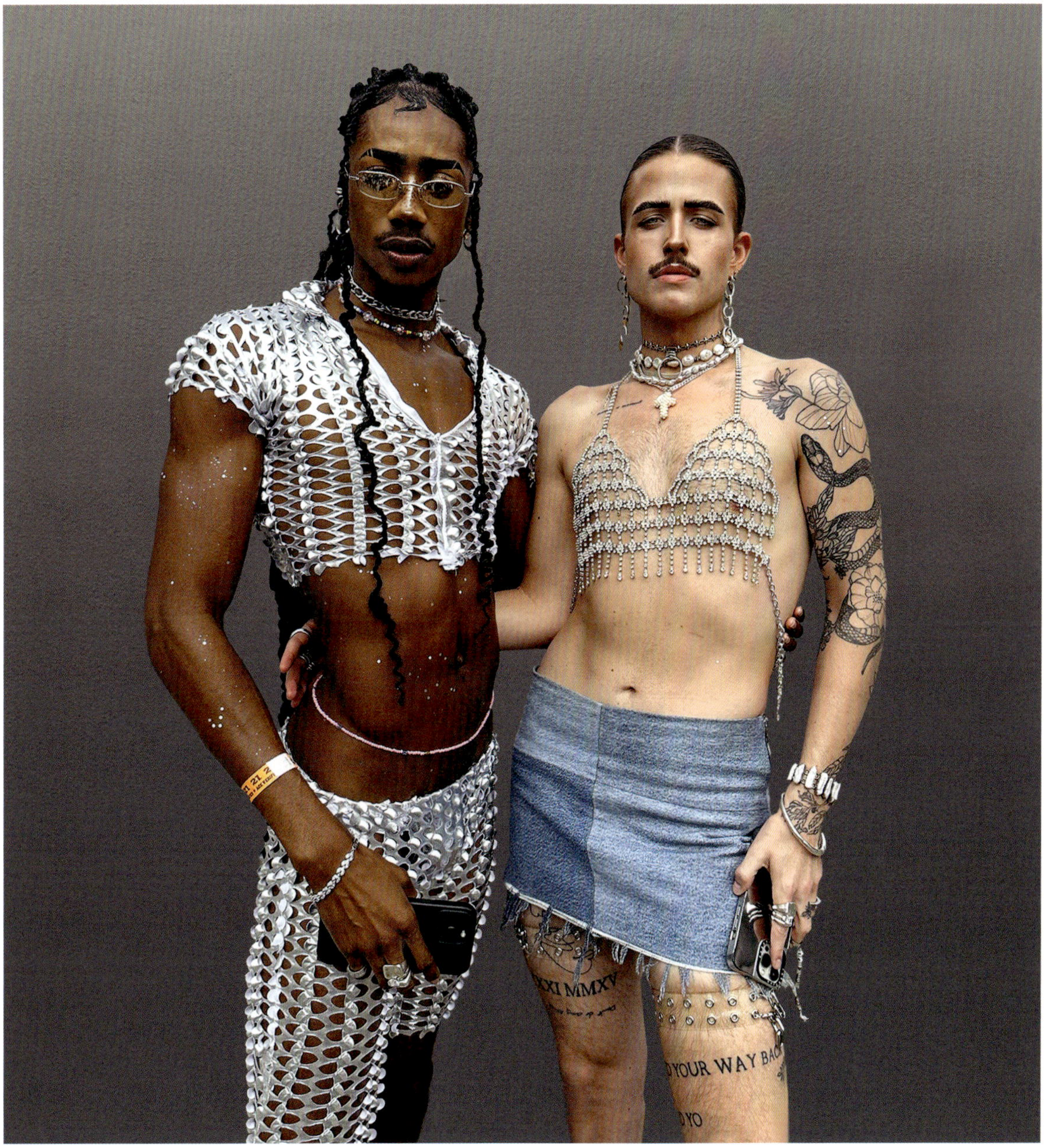
XXI MMXV
YOUR WAY BAC

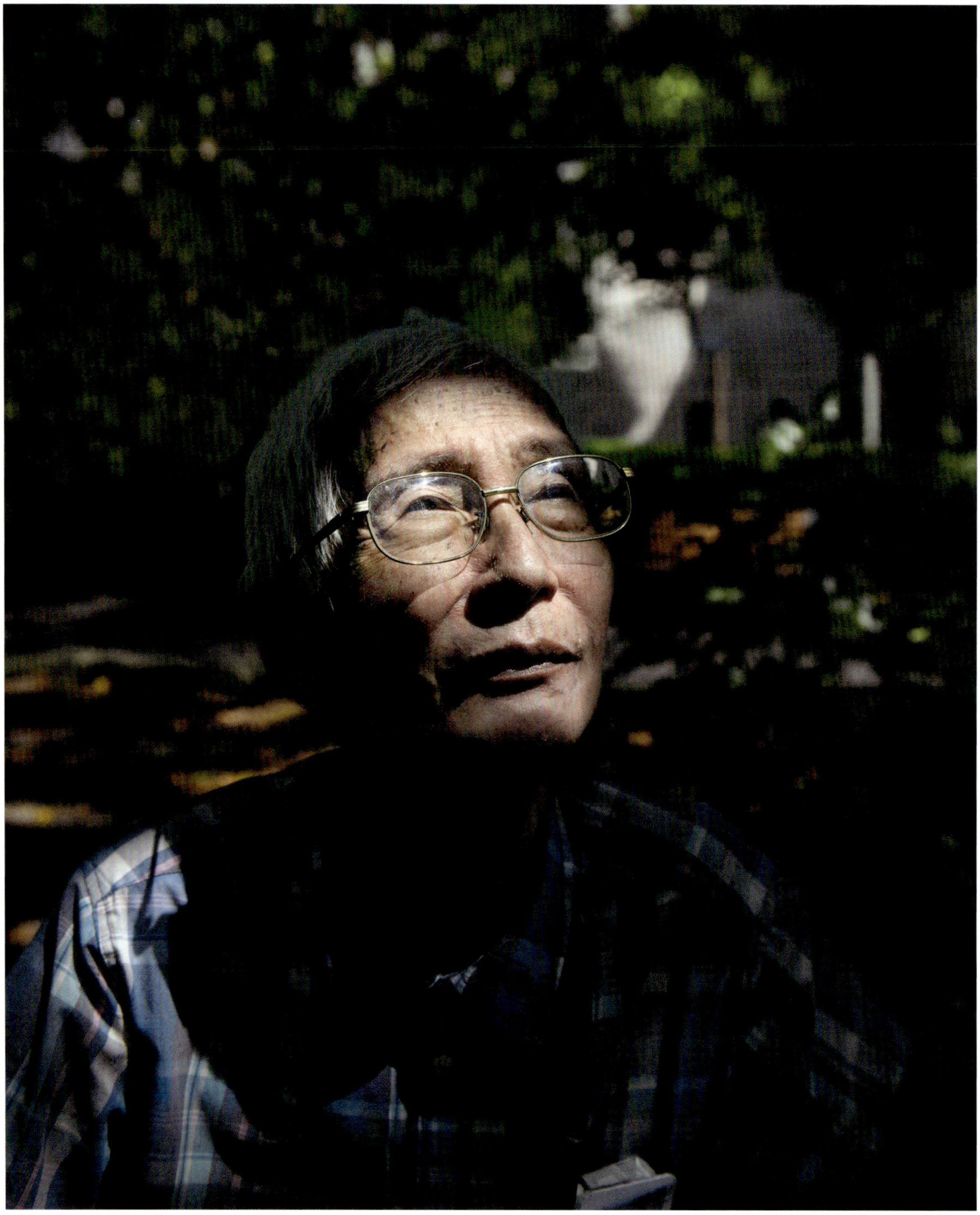

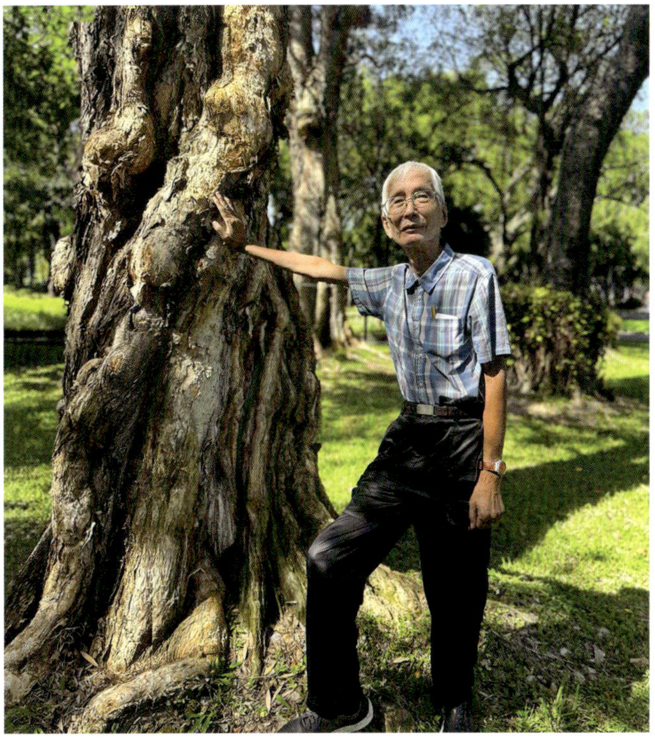

Mr. Chi 祁家威 | Taipei, Taiwan | 2023

Chi Chia-Wei was the first person in Taiwan to come out publicly as gay on national television in 1986. Named the 100 most influential people of 2020 by *Time* magazine, he is a symbol of hope for Taiwan's LGBTQ+ community, known for advocating marriage equality during a time when this could have led to imprisonment. His persistence in bringing the case to the courts eventually resulted in a landmark ruling by the Grand Justices, requiring the government to legalize same-sex marriage in 2019. Chi's courage has made him a prominent figure, standing against prejudice in the pursuit of equal rights.

Calvin and Clinton | San Francisco, CA | 2023

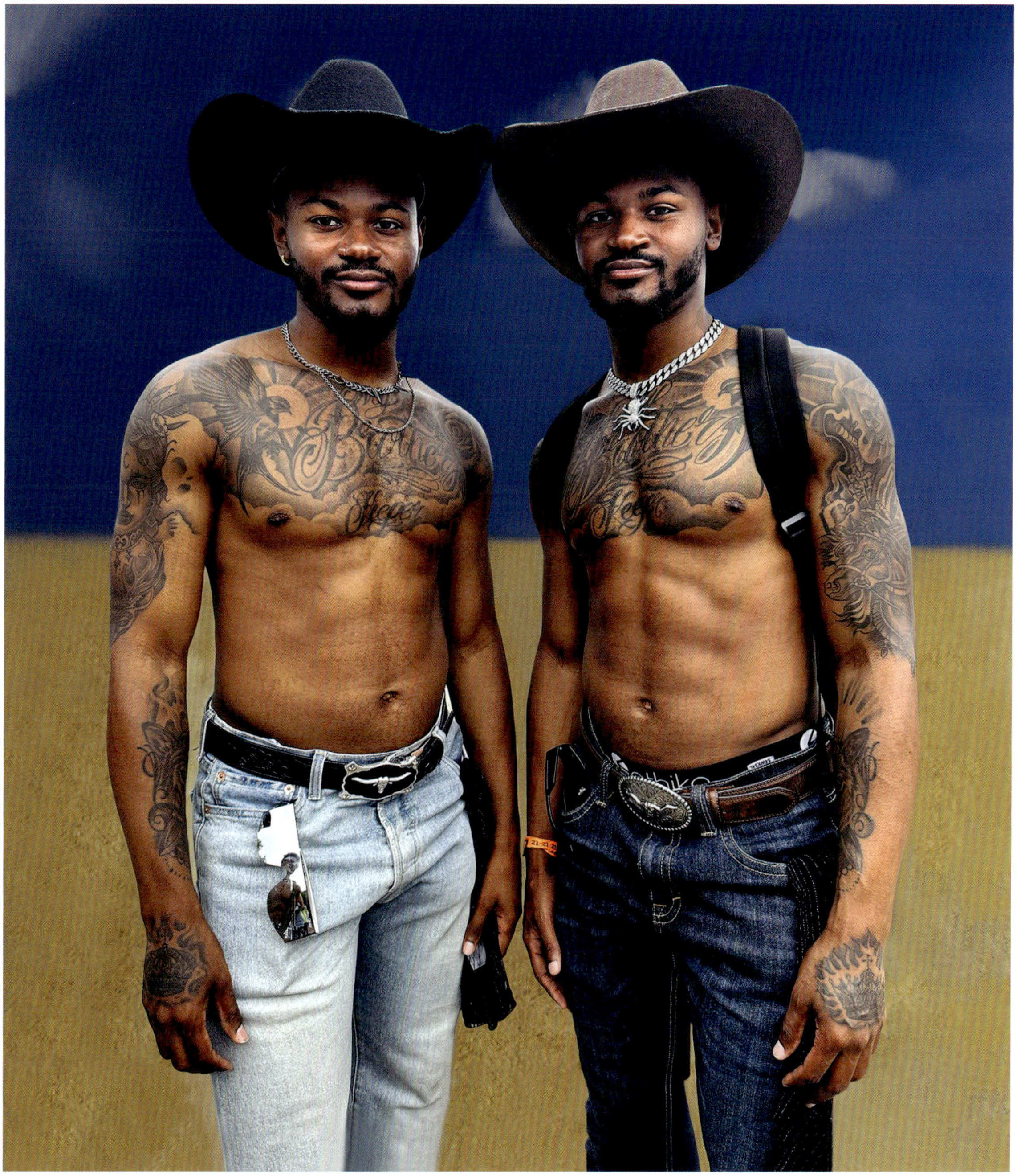

Nicole | San Francisco, CA | 2023

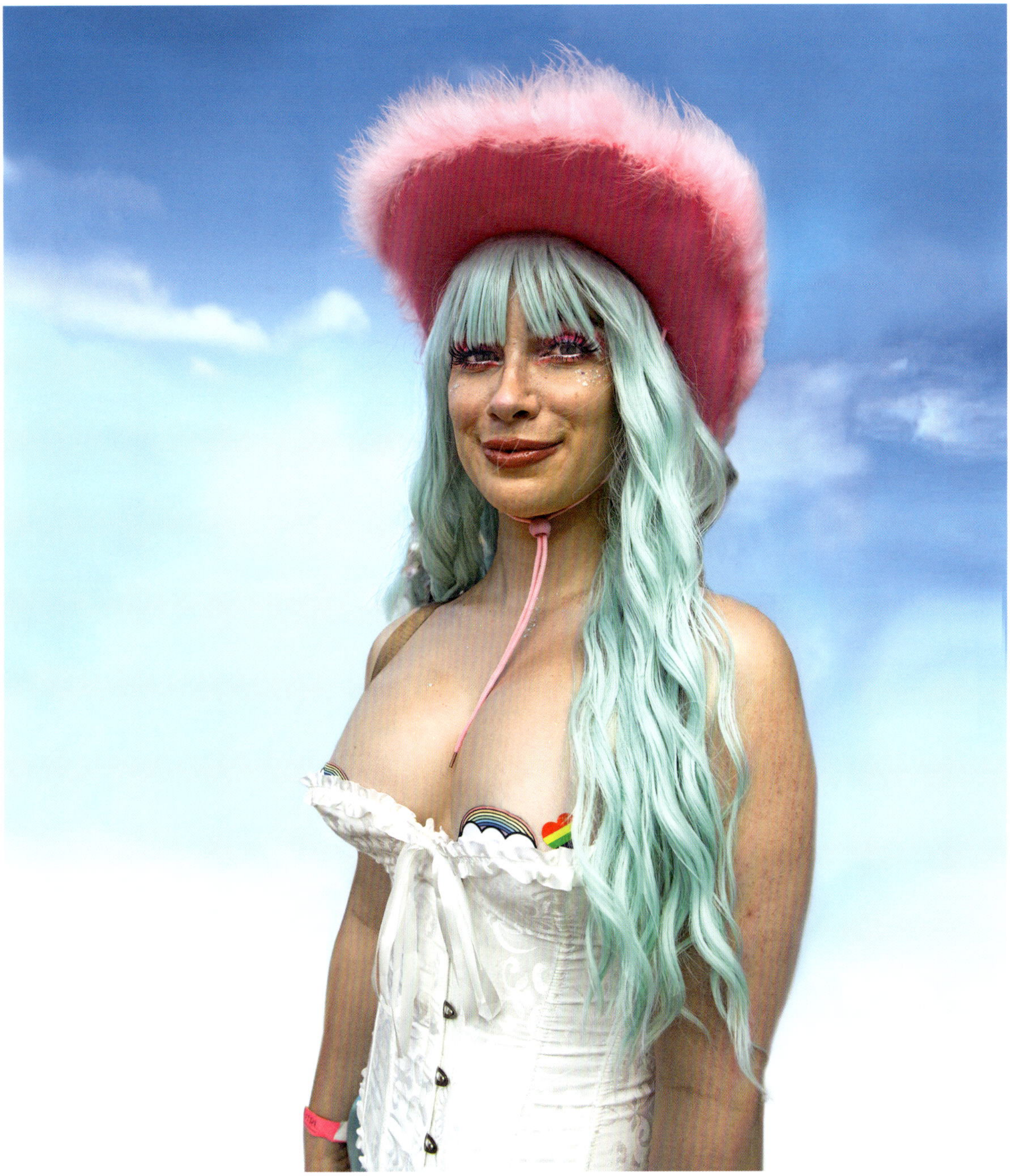

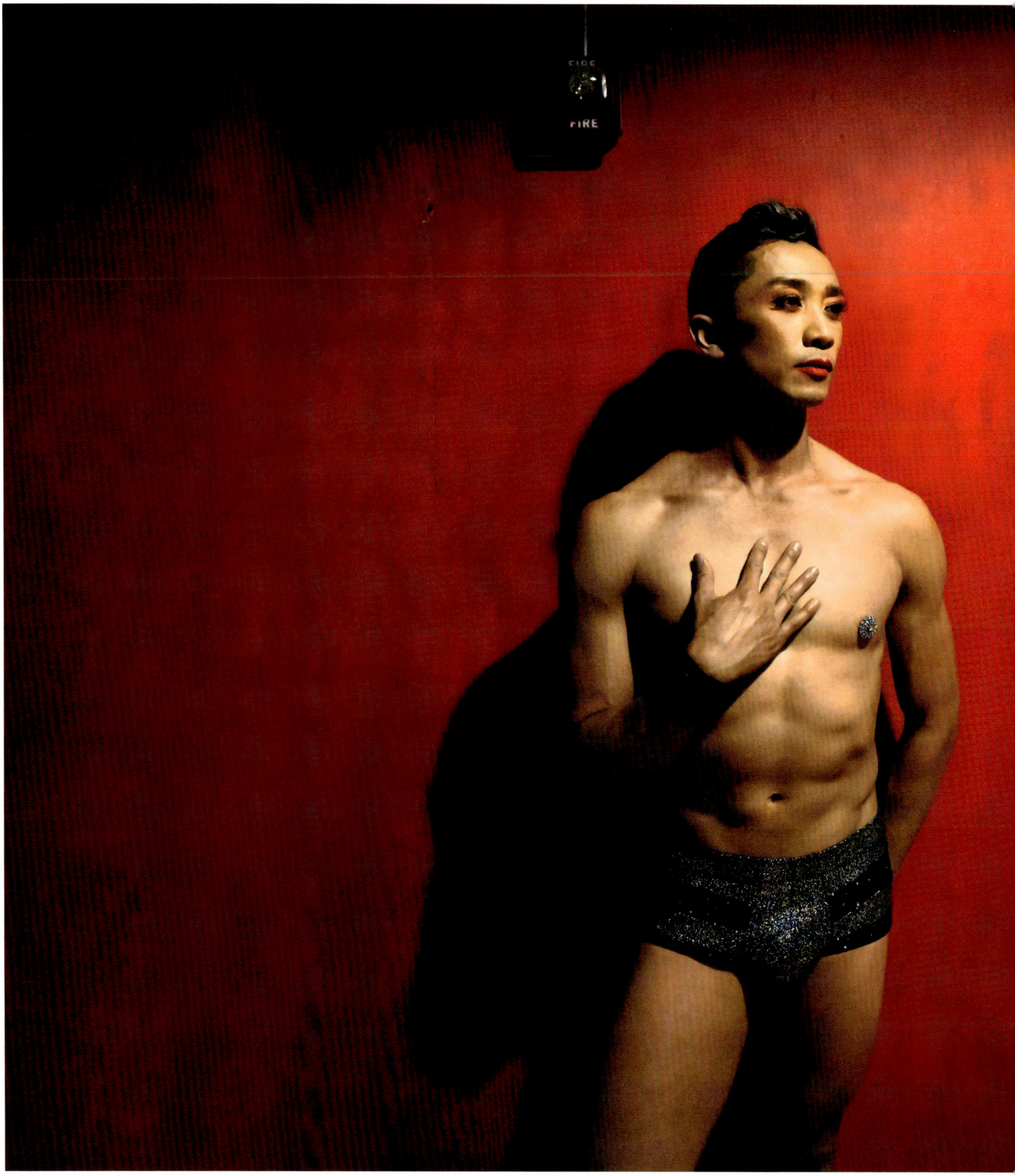
FIRE

David | San Francisco, CA | 2019

Jerremie | Denver, CO | 2023

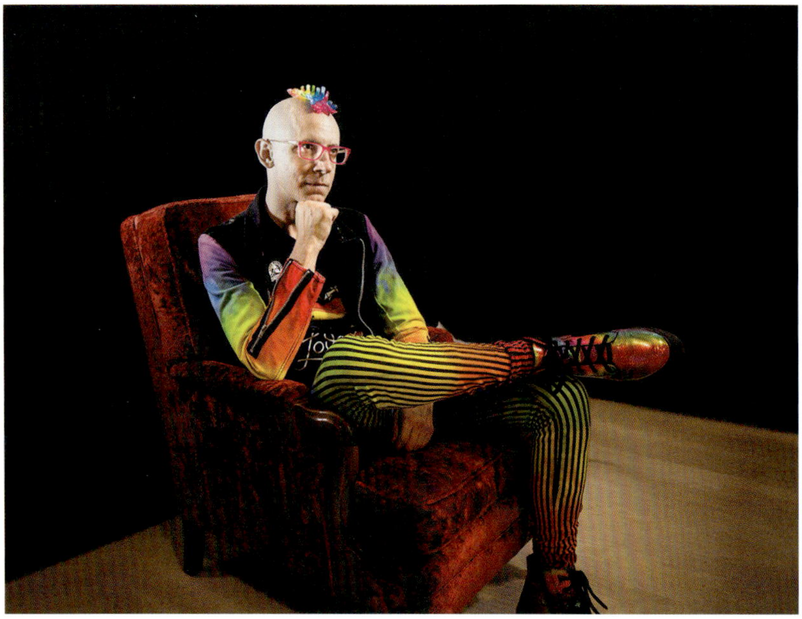

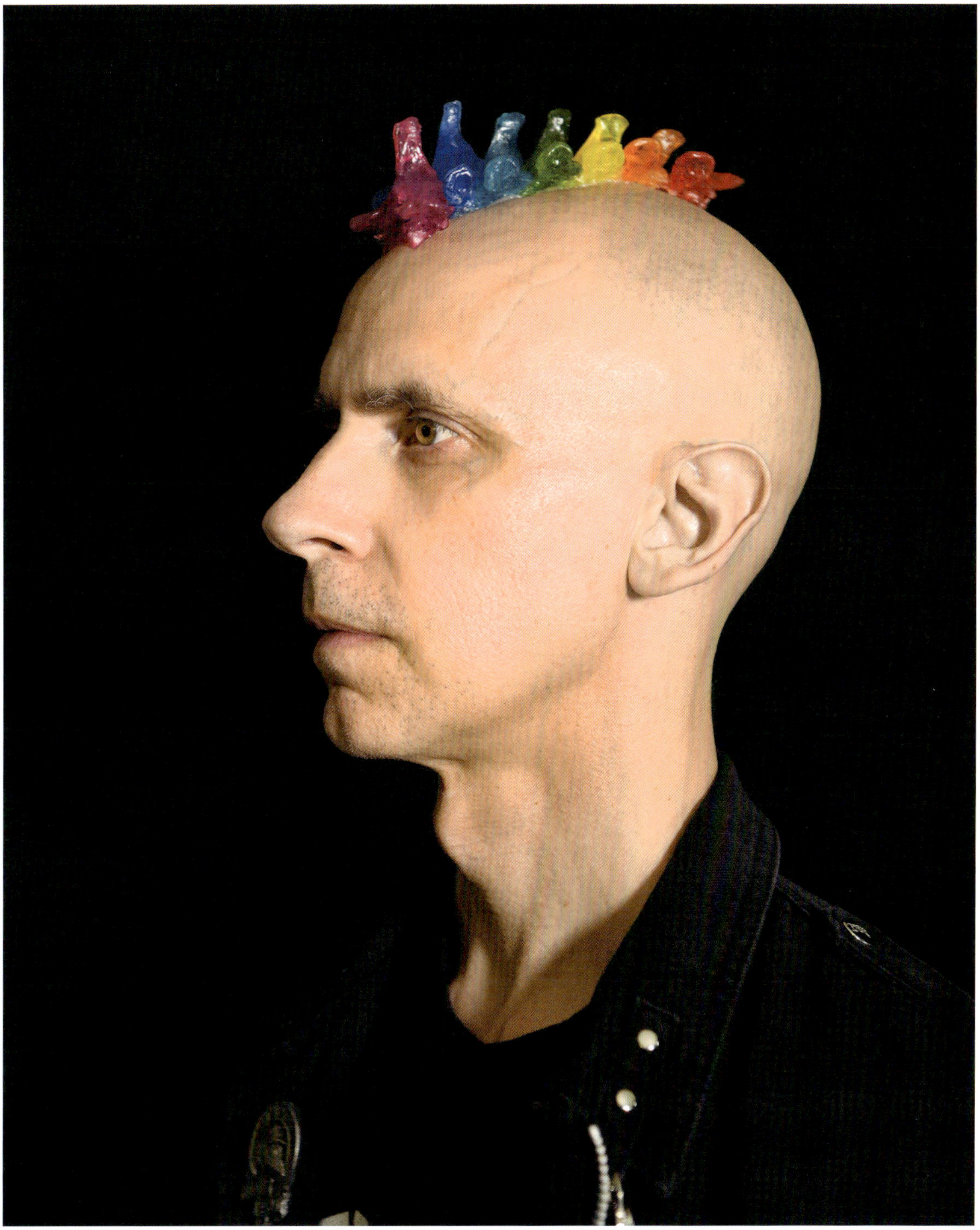

Kath, Theo, and Clay | Melbourne, Australia | 2023

"I grew up in a strictly Catholic household. Queerness was in no way part of my universe. Until I went to university. I hid it for years until I could move out of home. When I finally told my mum that I was a lesbian, the first words out of her mouth were: 'What about children?' My reply: 'I said I was a lesbian, Mum, not barren.' When I finally met my partner, Kath, and I told Mum that we were going to have kids, again she just couldn't fathom it. 'How do you suppose that will happen then?' she quipped. I didn't talk to her about it again after that. There were years of ups and downs of IVF. There was a year Mum spent with a stage 4 cancer diagnosis and chemotherapy. My mum died six weeks before we found out we were pregnant with our now four-year-old son. 'We did it, Mum,' I wish I could say to her. I wish she could have seen that queer doesn't exclude procreation. I wish our son had a grandmother.

Seventeen years we've been together. In a way it feels like forever. It's certainly been most of our adult lives. We met when I was doing my Ph.D. in Physics. Kath arrived at the university to work, having just completed her own Ph.D. in Physics. We sometimes joke around by saying, 'Excuse me, doctor, I need a consult over here. I think we should put more cheese on this pizza.' 'Why yes, doctor, I concur. It definitely needs more cheese.' With us both having strong backgrounds in science we find that we think the same way when it comes to problem-solving. With us both having had a decade of therapy, we've been able to help each other untangle the various traumas we entered the relationship with. I am one of six kids and Kath is one of four. For us, the idea of having a big family with lots of kids just seemed normal, and we talked about it for years. But after seventeen embryos were >>

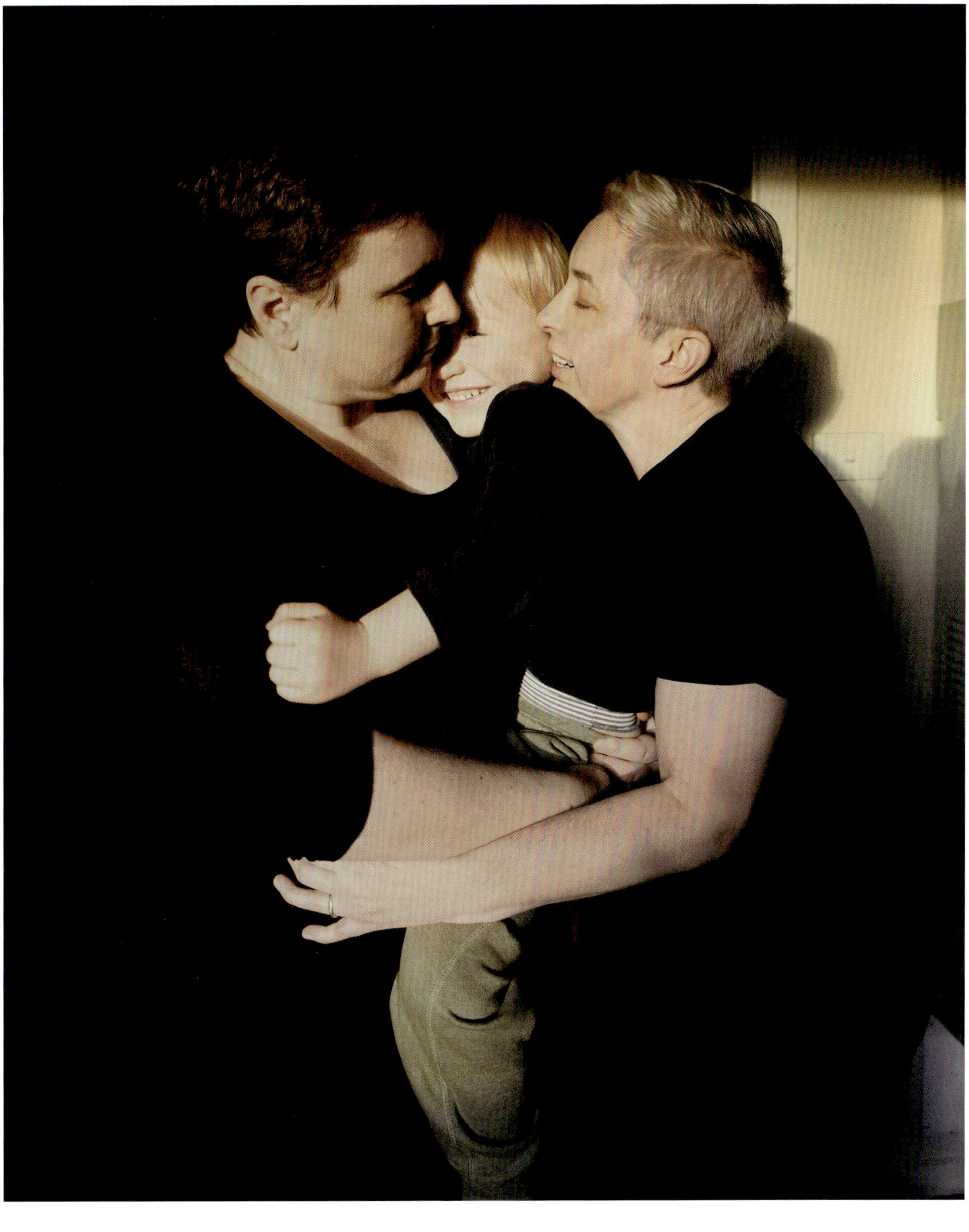

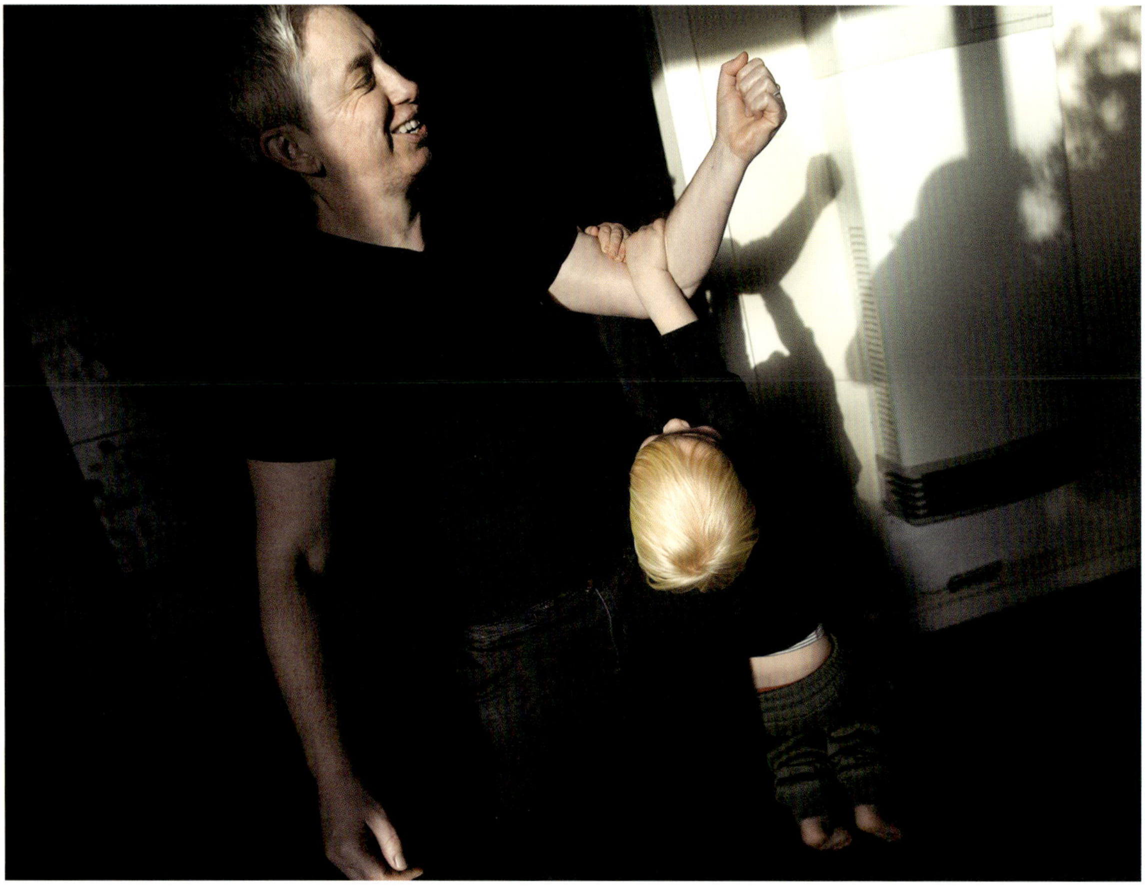

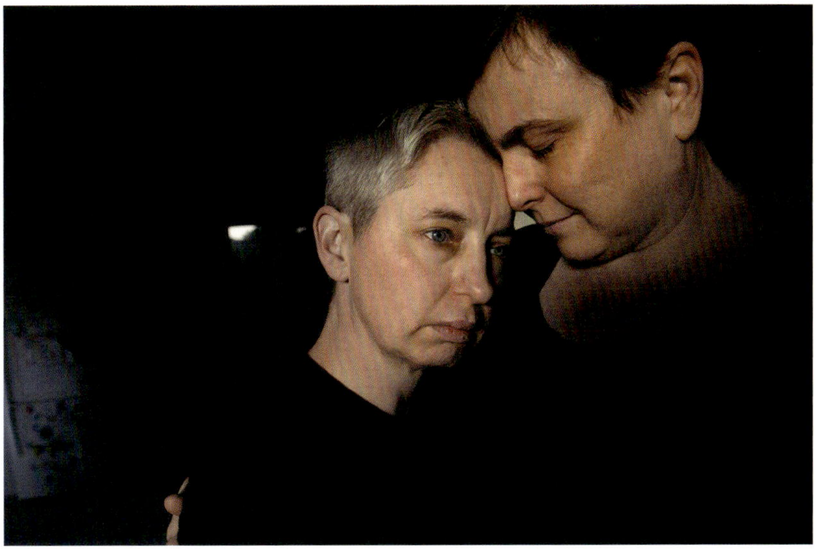

transferred into Kath,we finally had to call it quits and accept that we will be raising an only child. He was embryo number seven and he is the most precious thing in the world to us.

We got married ten years ago. A big wedding in a hall in a forest with the tallest of trees. All our family was there and our parents gave touching speeches. By this point, we had their support. It was a lot of work by them and a lot of patience from us that got them there. At the wedding, my five brothers met her three sisters and we all danced until midnight. Marriage wasn't legal, though, and at the time we didn't know when it would be. We just wanted our families to be one. On our fifth wedding anniversary we got legally married. Australia had just changed the law and we got to make our commitment to each other legally binding. The night before the much smaller ceremony at the registry office we'd done a pregnancy test, and that was Theo.

Over the many years Kath has helped me figure out many things about myself, most recently, my gender. As I transition increasingly further away from the painful "female" label into something much more masculine, something much more comfortable, she has shifted her words from 'You look pretty' to 'You look handsome.' That's about all that's changed between us really. That, and I'm just happier. That helps.

In just under a year we all got COVID, and Kath is still recovering. For her, Long COVID means not being able to run around with Theo or take him to the playground. Most days she struggles to do anything much but lie in bed. So my science career is on hold as I take the time to look after them. I would do anything for them. They are my world."—Clay

Ali | San Francisco, CA | 2022

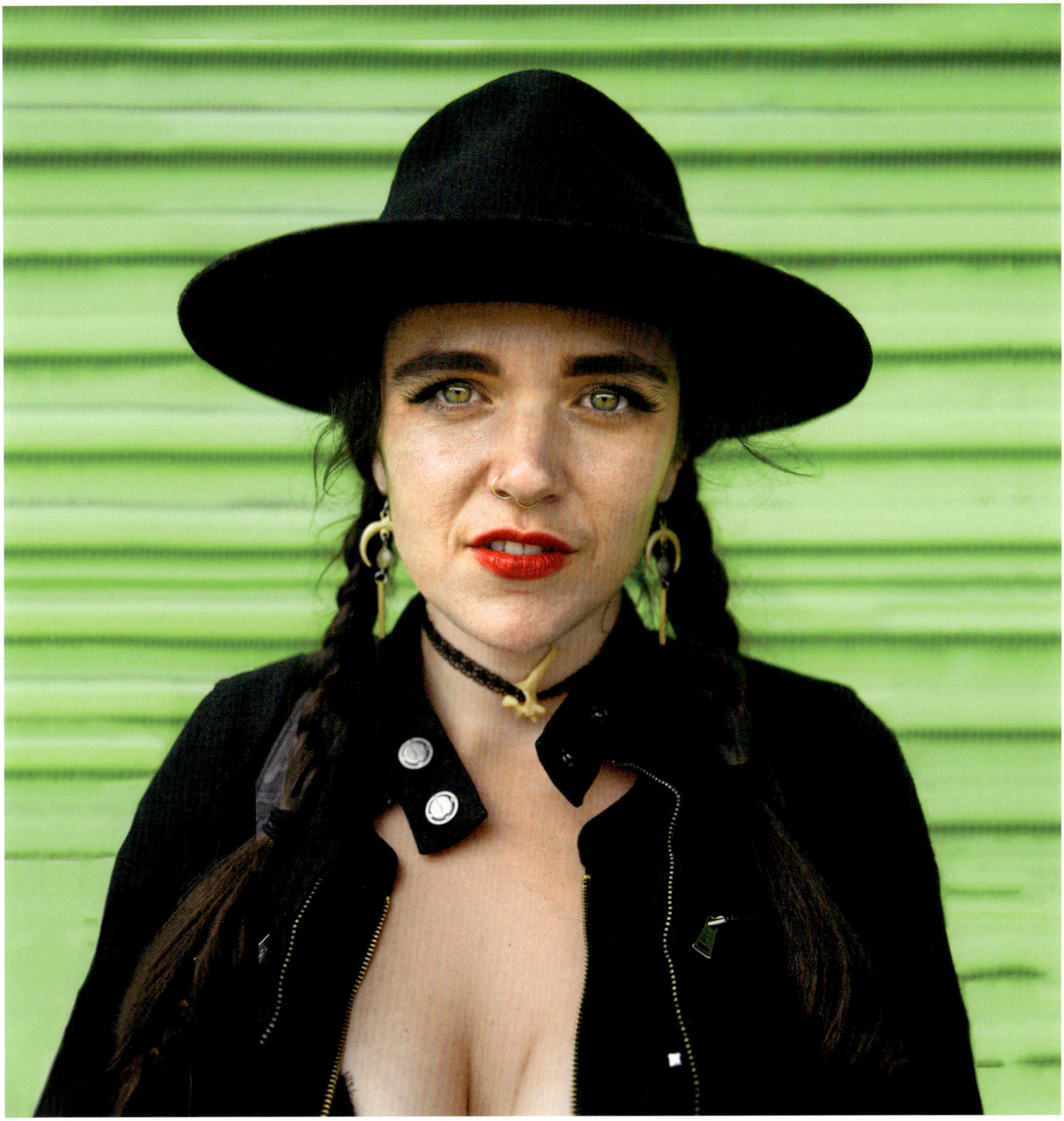

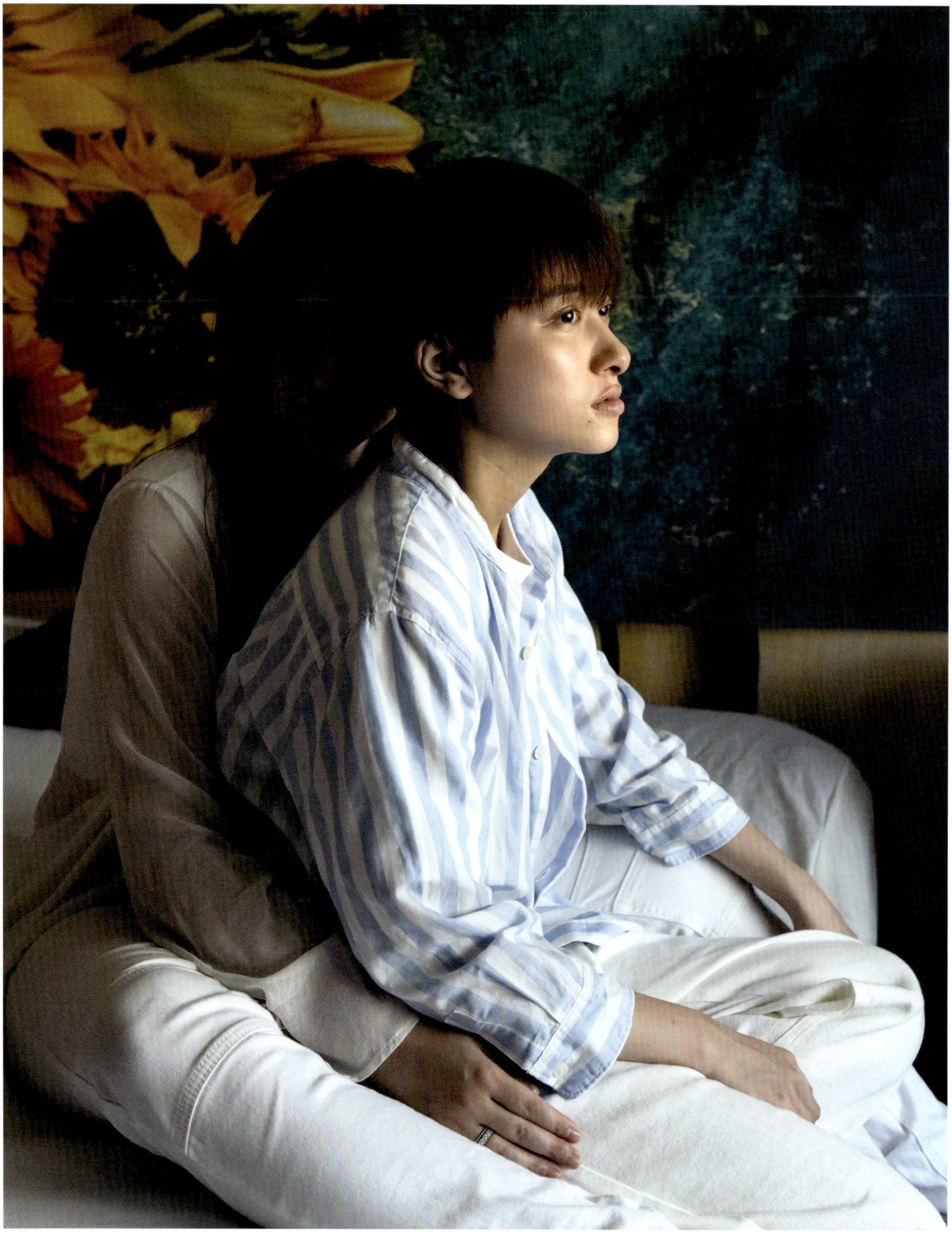

Jin Jin and Aky | Taipei, Taiwan | 2023

13歲國中一年級, 有一個女生很積極的追求我, 我一開始不知道我喜不喜歡她, 跟她說可以試試看在一起, 後來相處越久感覺越多～
有一天我帶那個女生回家過夜
我媽媽就直接問我他是你女友嗎?
我媽馬上知道也接受～ 他那時就希望我開心就好!

我很幸運沒有因為性向碰到什麼大問題, 可能因為我外表太明顯, 喜歡我的喜歡, 不喜歡的也不會找我

我跟Aky今年6/13登記結婚了
Aky之前在德國是訓犬師
來台灣後開始接觸演藝圈
—靚靚

"When I was thirteen years old and in the first grade of junior high school, there was a girl who was actively pursuing me. I didn't know if I liked her at first, so I told her that we could try being together. Later, the longer we got together, the more we felt for each other. One day I took that girl home to spend the night. My mother asked me directly if she was my girlfriend. My mother immediately knew and accepted it. She just wanted me to be happy!

I'm lucky that I haven't encountered any big problems because of my sexual orientation. Maybe it's because my appearance is too obvious. People won't come to me if they don't like me. Aky and I registered our marriage on June 13 this year."
—Jin Jin

"I never thought that my reason to remain in Taiwan would be love. I remember when I first came to Taiwan, I was with one of my ex-girlfriends who is Taiwanese and grew up in Germany. I fell in love with Taiwan: the culture, the nature, and the people. I really wanted to learn Chinese. So I waited some time, saved some money, and came to Taiwan all alone. It was difficult but luckily the LGBTQ community in Taiwan is very welcoming and I made friends almost immediately.

I didn't know that Taiwan is as open about the LGBTQ+ community as Western countries. It's amazing. I myself never struggled with hate here, other than in Germany where I had some not so nice experiences.

Jin and I came out around the same age: thirteen. We had some similar experiences. Our mothers were okay with it, unlike our fathers in the beginning. My father never liked the queer community, but when I came out to him, he said he needed some time to think about it. He somehow came around and said, 'He also prefers women.' I think he wanted to say that it's fine for him. Jin's father needed some more time. Time went by, and then once when he was drunk, he pulled Jin over and said that he had more girls than Jin. I guess that was also a kind of OK.

Some of our grandparents know it now as well. While mine came around eventually, Jin's grandmother still completely avoids talking about it and her grandfather still doesn't know yet. I really hope that will change someday, but until then we will keep living our loving life. We will keep spreading love and awareness of the of LGBTQ+ community and help each other to make this world a better place."—Aky

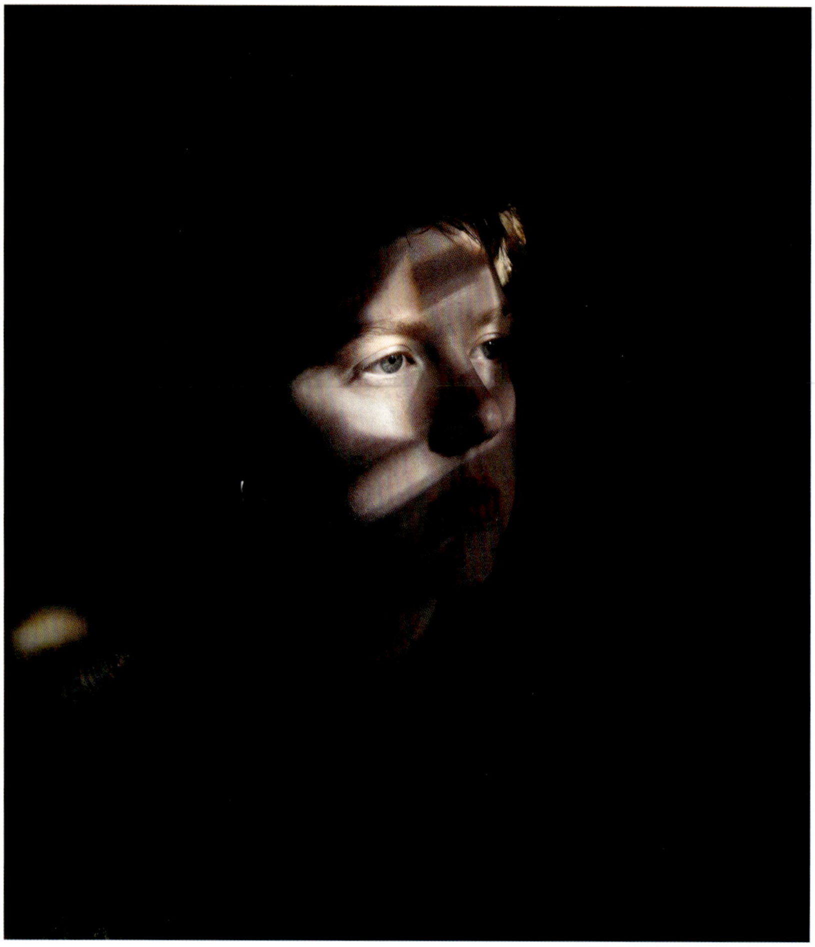

Charlie | Melbourne, Australia | 2023

Life – now

I'll wear nail polish,
and my heart on my sleeve.
And I'll wear bracelets made of beads
like the little girls do.

I'll have birthday cards with my name in them.
And I'll have a smile on my face,
and a prescription in my back pocket.

I'll hug my mum
and I'll dance in the pasta aisle.
I'll make hot tea with honey
and I'll watch my favourite films on repeat.
And I'll cry in the street,
so the little boys know it's okay.

I'll be the older brother
and I'll be the younger brother too.
And I'll cross the road at night,
so I'm not walking behind that girl.

I'll pick flowers that smell nice.
And I'll tell the people that are staring,
to pick their jaws up off the floor.

I'll watch the little girl next door,
As she shows me how fast she is.
And she'll tell me that she likes me,
Even though she doesn't like the other boys.

We'll dance in the lounge room
and we'll talk about outer space.
I'll be the asteroid.
And you'll be the dinosaur.
And I'll wear nail polish,
and my heart on my sleeve.
We'll wave at the people
in our favourite cars.
And, if I need to,
I will wave goodbye to you.
—Charlie

Lucie | Melbourne, Australia | 2023

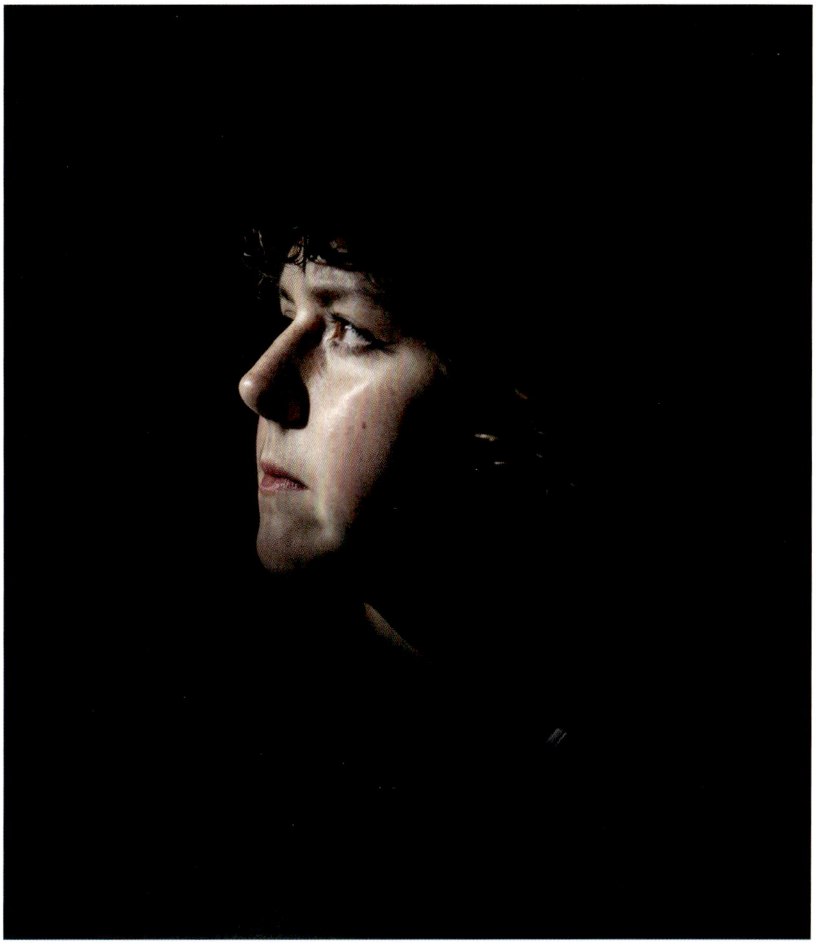

"My queerness slowly evolved. Growing into itself as the queer community around me grew out. My queerness is in a constant state of becoming."—Lucie

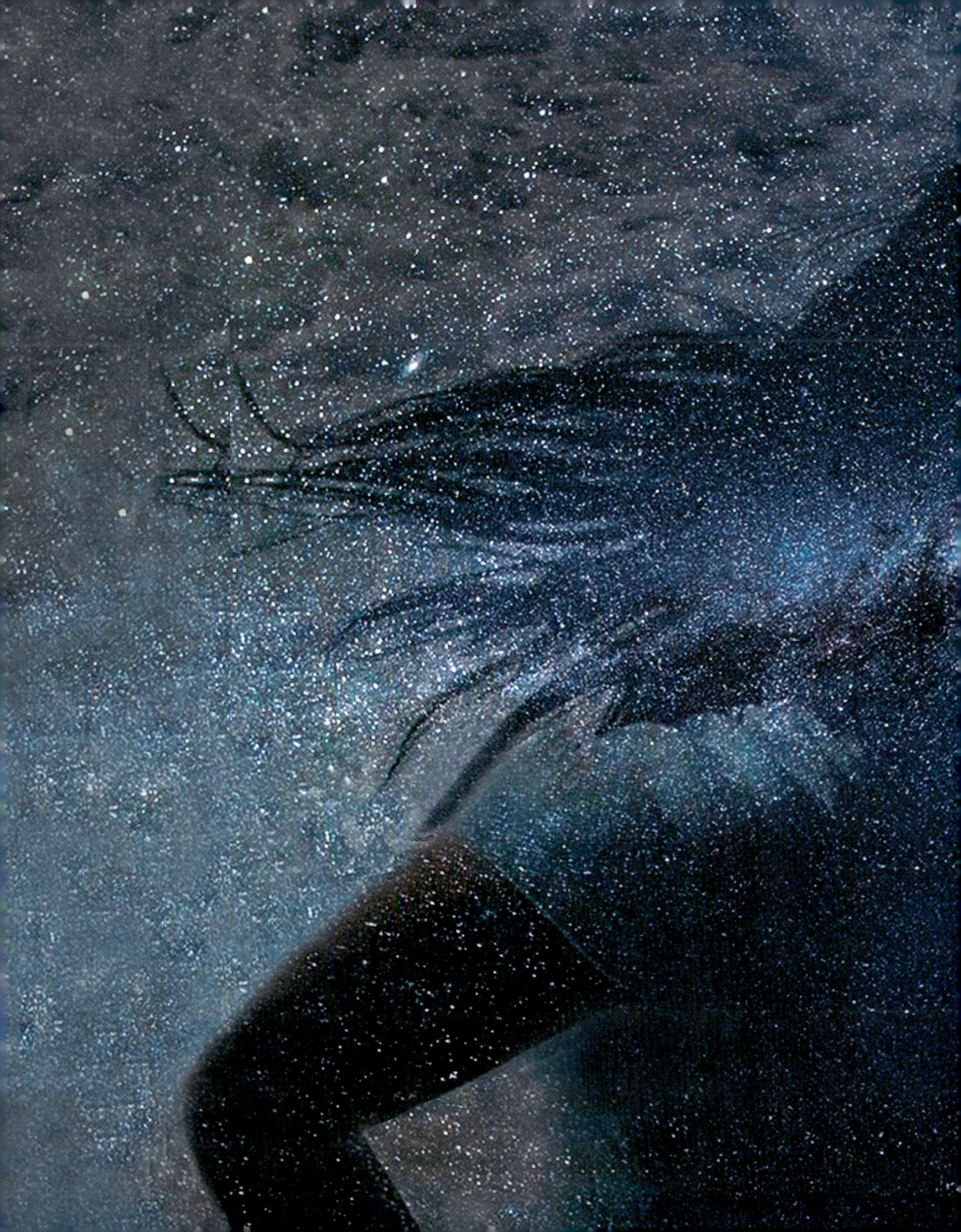

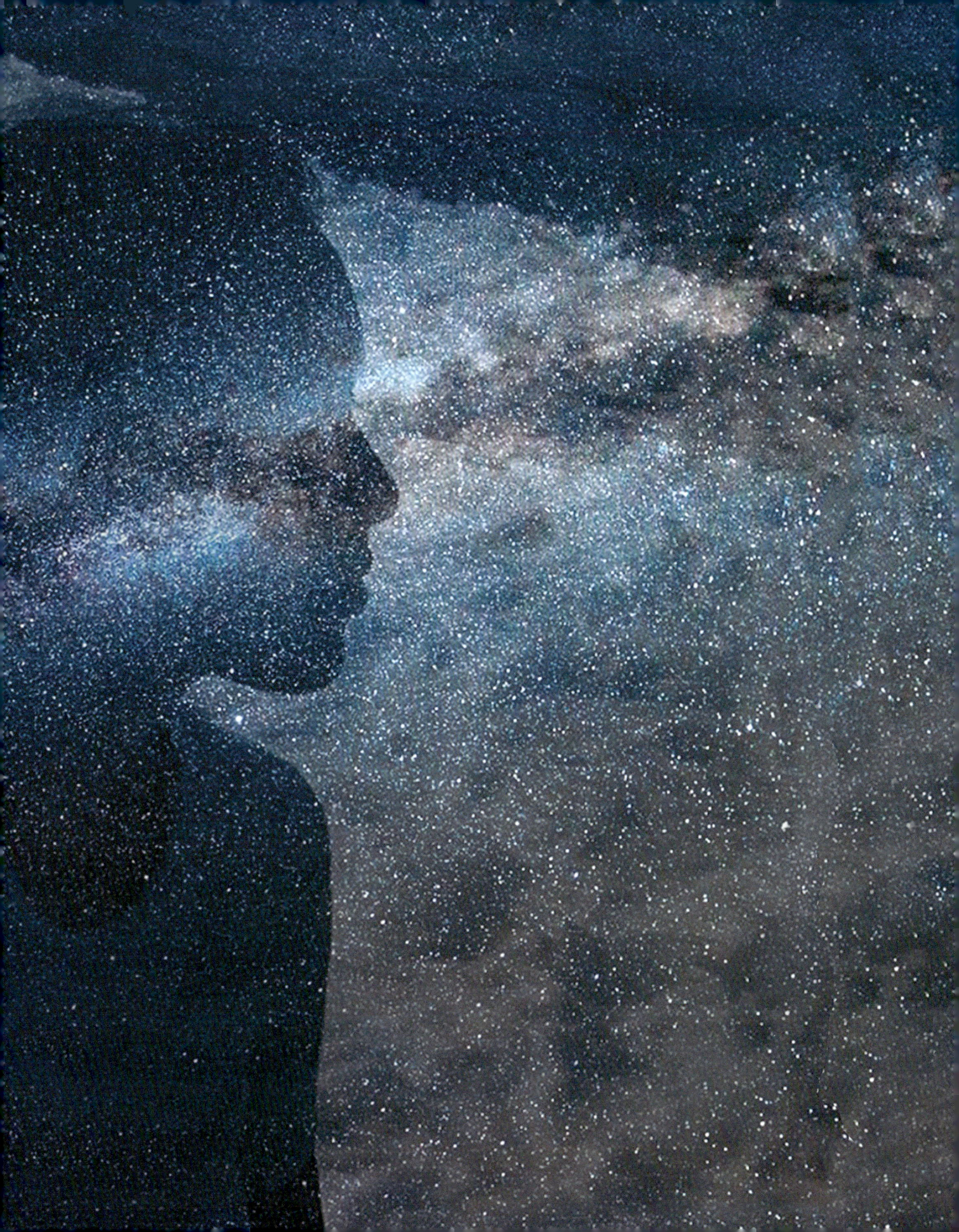

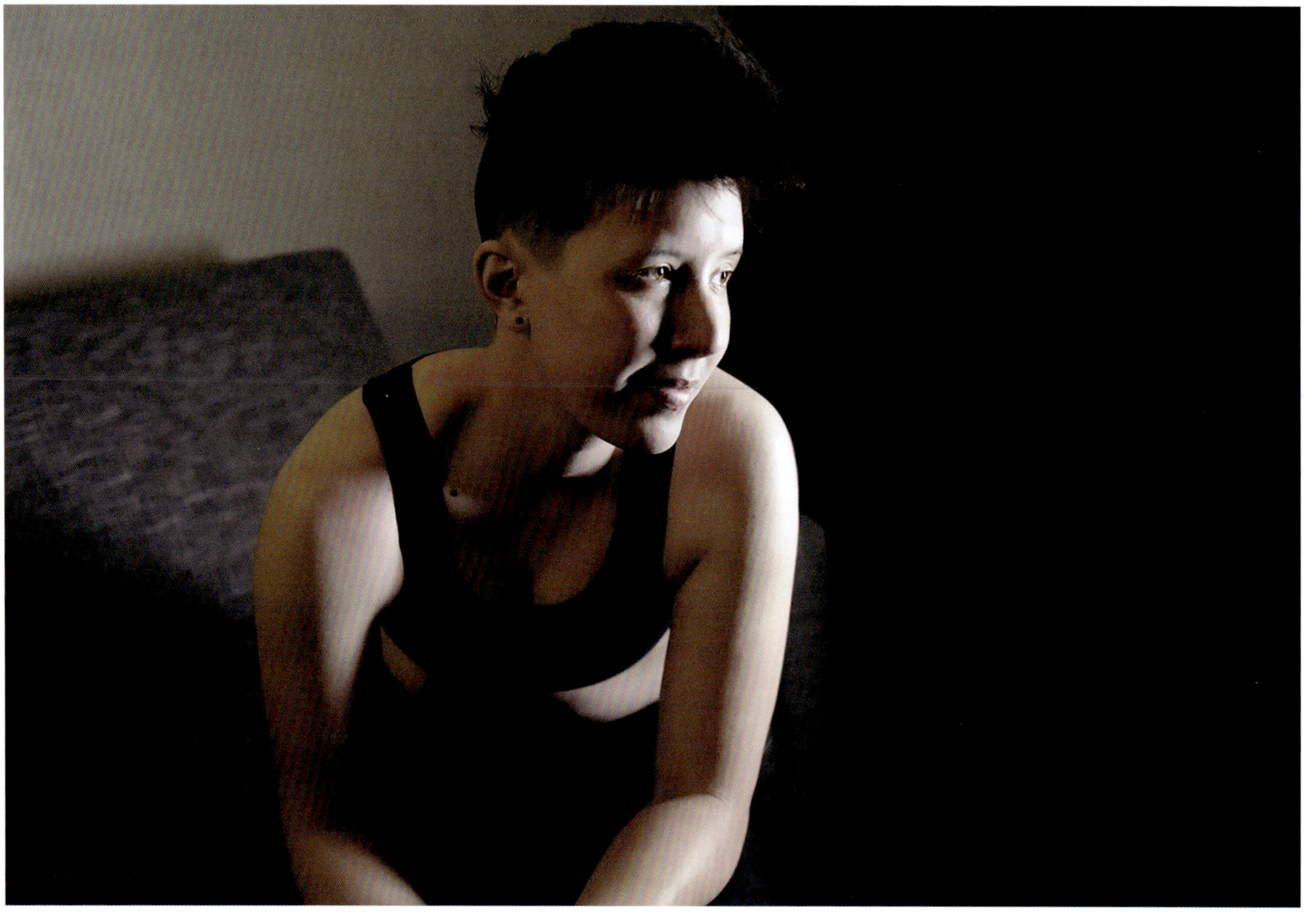

"I remember watching *Boys Don't Cry* when I was a child and sitting paralyzed in fear. The movie, based on a true story, is about a closeted trans man, Brandon Teena, in Falls City, Nebraska. Throughout the film, Brandon is fleeing from the police, his presumably transphobic family, and the men he met in bars who come after him when they find out he is trans. He is in hiding. He steals tampons from the gas station to evade questions. He hides the court summons that lists his legal name from his friends. Throughout the film we are made to feel that something bad is going to happen, that if and when these secrets come to light, they will bear tragic and irreparable repercussions. And they do. When Brandon is outed, he is raped and murdered. As a child, I watched in horror. My conclusion was that being gender non-conforming in the world meant grave consequences; that it was an abnormality that made you a target of violence.

Fast forward to today and we are still grappling with this type of representation in the media. And a lot of this representation is based on reality: transgender women of color are facing an epidemic of violence. In the most recent Pride month, in 2023, five black transgender women were murdered. We must bring attention to this injustice to make sure this doesn't continue to happen. And yet what does it do to us as a culture when the most common depictions of trans people are as victims?

I teach a college course called Introduction to Transgender Studies that predominantly consists of trans and queer students. In our discussions, the question of representation often comes up. One comment that sticks in my mind is from a student who shared how the media contributed their own fear to come out to their family. All they had seen in the media is that when you come out to your family as LGBTQ, you are

Lee and Sandra | San Francisco, CA | 2017

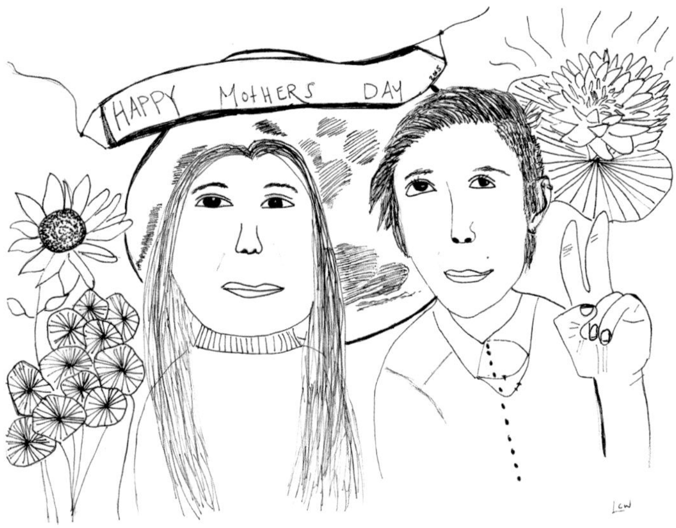

"A blessing and a perfect child. I was surprised when they came out to me only recently. We have always been very close and we will always be very close. My love for Lee is infinite and unconditional."
—Sandra

"I don't identify as a woman or a man. Like every gender that exists, my gender lies on a spectrum. To be honest, it wasn't until I was twenty-eight and I met other nonbinary trans people that I realized I was trans."
—Lee

immediately met with violence and rejection. When they came out to their parents, they were shocked when their parents didn't make a fuss about it. A big lesson we all reflected on that day was the danger of the single story. How many LGBTQ youth are hindered by the fear of rejection when that's the only outcome they have seen? I think we deserve more nuanced stories. We deserve to live full lives that are not determined by fear.

I have grown to believe that acceptance is more complicated than a simple binary of being accepted or being rejected. When I came out to my mom, she was confused. She questioned me because she didn't understand why I would date men until my early 20s only to suddenly become queer. Then, a couple years later, I came out as trans and nonbinary. This was another surprise for her since I presented feminine up until my twenties. I cut my hair short and started wearing baggier clothes and caps. I think what makes it hard for some parents is that we don't hear about a lot of stories of queer and trans people coming out in adulthood. And most of the stories we hear about queer and trans youth coming out are white.

It took time for my mom and me to come to a common understanding of my coming out process. We are still working on building this understanding. But my mom has been my most persistent supporter in my family. My other family, including my Jewish family on my father's side, have acknowledged my identity without saying much or asking me questions. It's an unspoken topic. Is this acceptance? I'm not sure. It's definitely not rejection. Many of my friends are pleasantly surprised to hear about how supportive my mom is. It is inspiring for others to see my Asian American mother supporting her queer and trans child, since we aren't represented in the media much at all. >>

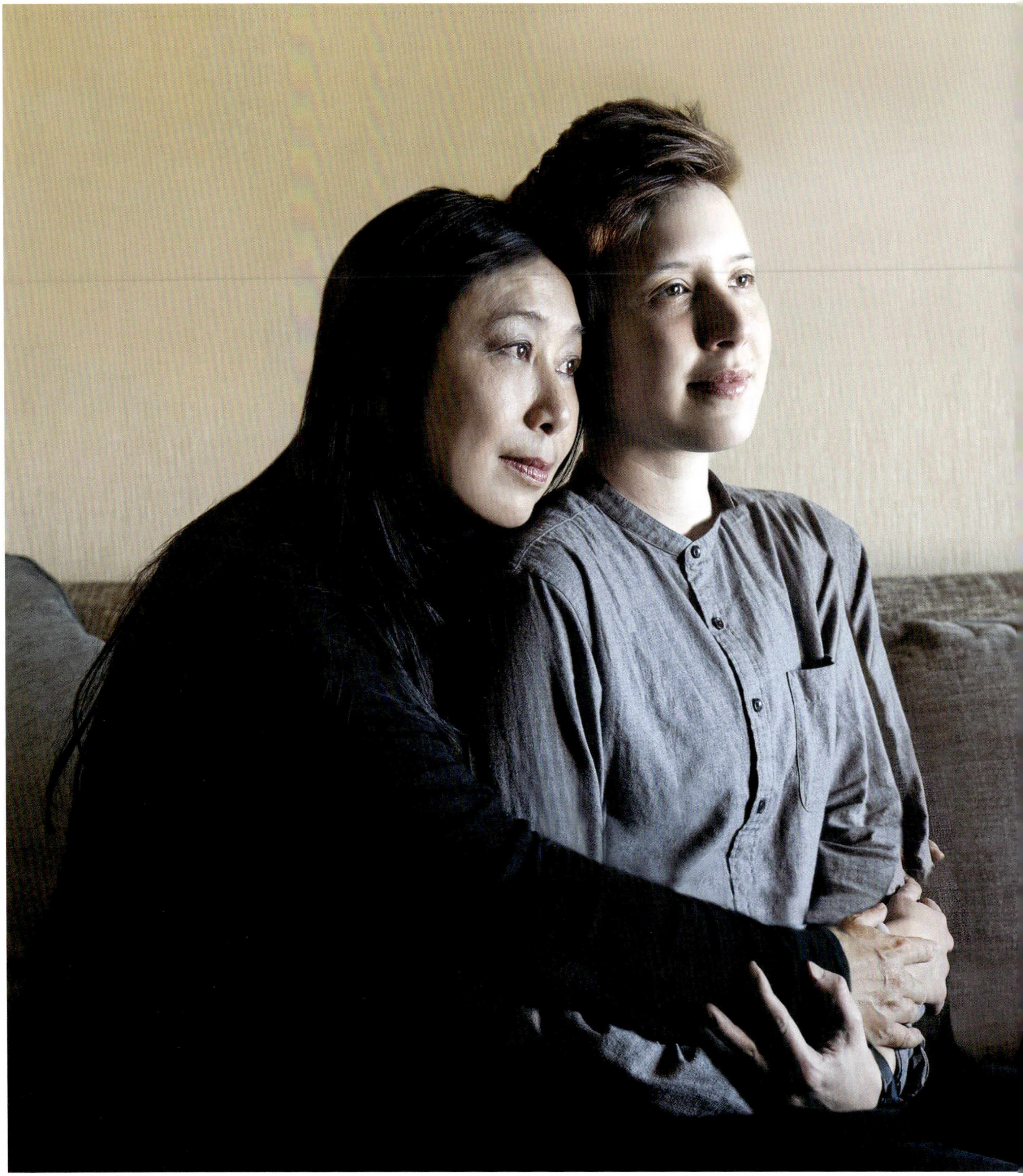

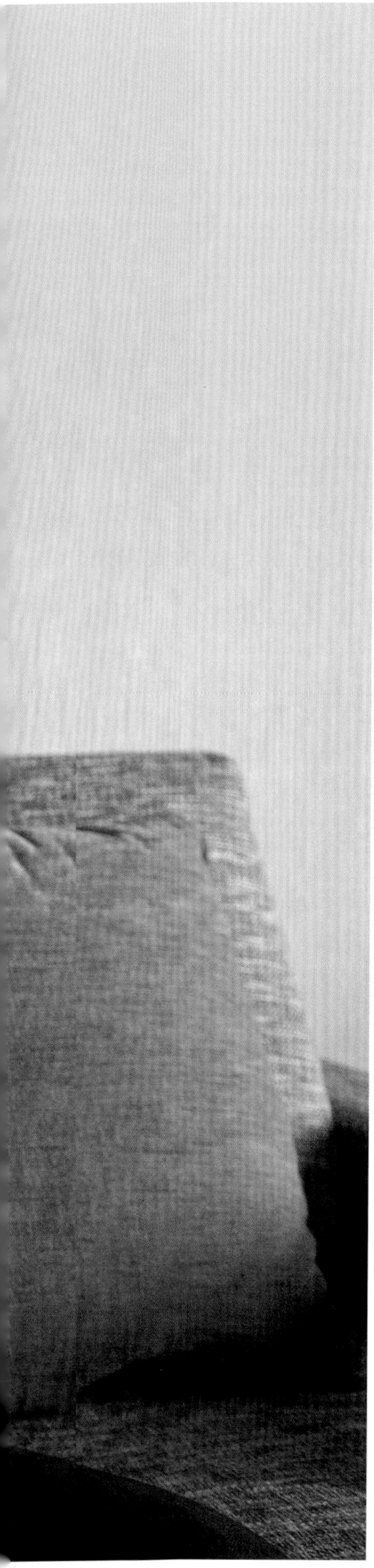

In my own process of self-discovery, I have needed a lot of space to figure myself out. And our parents are also in a process of self-discovery. Their own notion of gender as a constant is being contested. They may feel uneasy because they don't understand what their child is going through and they may feel that the connection they believed they shared as straight and cisgender people has been broken. On the flip side, some of us are lucky to have family who are dedicated to learning and processing these developments in their child's life.

We need more representation. More voices in the room. More nuanced depictions of our lives. We need more cisgender and straight people proclaiming their unwavering support for their LGBTQIA friends, family, and lovers. We need more cisgender and straight people who are ready to challenge homophobia and transphobia in the home and elsewhere."—Lee

Since they were born, Lee has lived a a life of many different experiences. When they were only two weeks old, we moved back to the United States because we were part of the U.S. foreign service, and they have since attended international schools in various countries.

"Lee received fellowships and scholarships, and they excelled as an all-star athlete and musician. I was always a proud mom not just because of their outstanding achievements, but most importantly, Lee has always remained grounded and they have helped many others in their personal struggles or with their academics. I was surprised when Lee came out as non-binary when they were twenty-eight. I have close gay friends and I have worked on photo projects on the LGBTQA+ community, and I was quick to to embrace Lee's identity. Even so, I was learning to understand how difficult it must be to make this statement, to challenge all the obstacles it may lead to. Lee won't be alone. I will always support them.

Lee has inspired me to create a portfolio of photographs that has been immensely important to our lives. Many appear in these pages. I hope we can continue to push back against the neglect and intolerance of our often-prejudiced society."—Sandra

Acknowledgments

The photographs presented in this book were made possible by Jon Stryker: philanthropist, architect, and photography devotee.

This book was made possible in part by a grant from the Arcus Foundation*

This project is inspired by my child Lee. My deepest gratitude to Lee, Vikk Shayen, Takeki Sugiyama, Andreas Müller-Pohle, Elizabeth Avedon, Cynthia Chin-Lee, Virginia Heckert, Kevin Yang, Lai Wen Wei, Midori Kawamukai, Stella Kramer, Susan Meiselas, Alyssa Coppelman, Molly Roberts, and Sarah Leen.

Special thanks to my subjects and rainbow families for their love, trust, and openness to tell their stories to me for inclusion in this book:

United States: Lee, Keith, Asher and Hart, Leo and Judy, Austin, Barbara and Jess, Jon and Mikael, Jeffrey and Amelea, Olivia, Alexis and Irma, Brett and Sarah, Kathy, Alex, Lee, Alexander and Alejandro, Thai, David N, Ceraun, Ariel, Aly and Amara, Lauren, Emmet, Davey, Daenara, Ari, Allan, Hiroki and Desun, Ethan, Cari, Adam, Jerremie, Doug and Jeff, Mono and Elian, Ali, Calvin and Clinton, Kyle, Michael and Kaden, Marianne, Nicole; **Taiwan**: Chi Chia-Wei, Wei and Vivian, Sanna and Barkley, Jin Jin and Aky; **Australia**: Clay, Kath and Theo, Kim and July, Charlie and Lucie; **Iceland**: Sadie, David Iñiguez, Margrét, Arna.

I would like to extend my special gratitude to Jurek Wajdowicz of Emerson, Wajdowicz Studio for believing in my work and offering me this amazing opportunity. Jurek's dedication and supportive art direction helped to bring the concept of this book into reality. To his creative team Lisa LaRochelle and Yoko Yoshida-Carrera and to New Press editor Ben Woodward, a big thanks for the great collaboration on this project.

Finally, I would like to express my heartfelt thanks to Carol McCusker's eloquent and captivating introduction, "The Power of Us."

*The Arcus Foundation is a global foundation dedicated to the idea that people can live in harmony with one another and the natural world. The Foundation works to advance respect for diversity among peoples and in nature (www.ArcusFoundation.org).